All to All

Brian P. McKeon

Cover design by Grace Milburn Viertel.

ISBN:1512047988
ISBN-13:9781512047981

DEDICATION

Christ my Savior: For from him and through him and to him are all things. To him be glory forever. Amen.

To Hellen, Niya, and Sameera.

To all those who have wandered down the road of life with me.

CONTENTS

ACKNOWLEDGMENTS

I have to start with my wife and children, because they inspire me to be better. I did not get married until I was in my thirties, and there came a time where I thought I would never have my own children. I am so grateful to God for the gift of family. My parents gave me an incredible gift in bringing me up in the Word, and sacrificing so much to make sure I had a good education and solid foundation. I am also grateful to them for letting me take off to see and explore what God was calling me to. I think also of the valuable lessons I am still learning from my in-laws, the Matetes.

Danny and Mary Pat Mitchell have done so much work in helping this book actually happen, and I truly appreciate them. The Board of R3 International not only for encouraging me to write this all down, but also for the roles they have played in helping see the work and ministry of R3I continue.

I think of so many that have mentored me and helped me understand both the practical outworking of the teachings of the Scriptures and the complexities of doing cross cultural ministry. The various Pastors who have shepherded me over the years: Michael Alford, Randy Nabors, Mike Higgins, Kevin Smith, Calvin Jett, Bill Dages, Joe Muutuki, Imbumi Makuku, Titus Baraka, and others.

CHAPTER 1

INTRODUCTION

How can I, as a middle class American, effectively do cross cultural work today? This is the question that I have been asking for a number of years, and for which I am attempting to spell out an answer. I began doing missions work as a teenager, and in the twenty-plus years since my first trip, have travelled to over forty countries, run an international disaster response organization, worked in intentionally diverse ministries, and married across racial and cultural lines.

I sat with an old man in East Africa, a man who was a ministry leader, well-respected, and someone for whom I personally had a great deal of admiration. I was travelling quite a bit in those days, and had made it a point to ask people about how I should be going about the work of missions and ministry in this day and age. "Anytime I talk to a white man, I automatically revert to a submissive mode. It was so drilled into us in the old days, and it has never gone away," he said, and wiped a tear from his eye. We were sitting in a roadside shop, eating chicken, and it was both dusty and sunny, so maybe some dust had gotten in his eye. He was about fifty years older than me, and we had made a habit of grabbing lunch together when I was in town. I had finally asked him that question that had bothered me for many years, and it had taken patience for us to reach the relational level for him to answer without inhibition. The question that I asked him, and many others, was simply this: "How should we, as foreigners, as Americans, do missions today?"

The question started on one of my first-ever missions trips, as a high school student. We were travelling through one African country to reach another, and stopped in a small town. One of the leaders of the group knew a missionary in that town, and so some of us went to their home for dinner. I sat in shock as this missionary rattled off racist comments, showing little love or respect for the culture or people he was called to serve. This was not the last time I would hear a missionary or American Christian ministry leader make comments like this. Over the next twenty years I would hear similar comments and see such attitudes reflected in actions. I would also hear the pain of the local church and ministry leaders at being treated and talked about in this way. I saw paternalistic, condescending, and even racist attitudes, not just in some backwater church or from some "good old boy," but on the front lines of the mission field, in some of the nicest churches in America, and from the mouths of people with advanced degrees and powerful reputations.

There is something in my personality that often leads people to believe I am on their side, in agreement with them. I am told I nod my head often, which to me is a sign that I hear what they are saying, but seems to convey agreement. This opens the door for people to say what they really think, which works both ways; I hear things I really don't like, but also am privy to thoughts that are rarely verbalized. I have learned to listen and though I can't always keep my mouth shut, I am able to do so often enough to be able to come at this conversation having heard multiple perspectives.

On a number of occasions I have had older African men share their stories, and seen the pain in their eyes. They are stories of lies, discrimination, and degradation. Too often the stories about how Africans are treated by white people are negative, though I have heard some amazing positive tales as well. Often it is a mixture of both: the missionary who constantly treats the young indigenous church leader in a patronizing manner can be the first to give money when there is a genuine need.

My hope is that I can help us collectively do a better job of developing biblical connections across cultural lines. Many of my stories will have taken place on the mission field, but I am not against missionaries or missions, I want to be clear on that. Some of my best friends are missionaries and I hold them in the highest regard. Many are heroes of the faith, and like all of us, imperfect and unsanctified in some areas of their lives. The guy who makes the racist joke in the prayer meeting is the same one who recently risked his life to give medical treatment in an extreme situation, the arrogant missionary up front is at the home of the offended church staff member the following week begging forgiveness. We are not perfect, and I am in no way advocating an abandonment of the pursuit of global missions, but rather a change in the way we think about our brothers and sisters around the globe. I have spent much of my time in Africa, and have tremendous connections there, but some of my stories come from other parts of the world; the basic concepts here are applicable everywhere, to anyone working across cultural lines, even in the U.S. as we see continued strife between white and black in our own cities.

Some of this may be intimidating, or may seem like too much. You may also find yourself asking whether you can really do these things. Most of the lessons I have learned have been because I messed up. You will too, and that is okay. 2 Peter 1:3-10 gives some good encouragement, both as to why we should try to do better, and also in persevering:

"His divine power has granted to us all things that pertain to life and godliness, through the knowledge of him who called us to his own glory and excellence by which he has granted to us his precious and very great promises, so that through them you may become partakers of the divine nature, having escaped from the corruption that is in the world because of sinful desire. For this very reason, make every effort to supplement your faith with virtue, and virtue with knowledge, and knowledge with self-control, and self-control with steadfastness, and steadfastness with godliness, and godliness with brotherly affection, and brotherly affection with love. [8] For if these qualities are yours and are increasing, they keep you from being ineffective or unfruitful in the knowledge of our Lord Jesus Christ. For whoever lacks these qualities is so nearsighted that he is blind, having forgotten that he was cleansed from his former sins. Therefore, brothers, be all the more diligent to confirm your calling and election, for if you practice these qualities you will never fall." [i]

The challenge here is not to stop, but to do it better.

As Christians, we should constantly be examining our own hearts to see what wicked ways are in us, and any thoughts or behaviors in us that can hamper our opportunities for discipleship should be adjusted. This is not a book for only missionaries or church workers. It contains general principles that can be implemented in any cross cultural scenario.

CHAPTER 2

WHAT YOU BELIEVE IMPACTS HOW YOU RESPOND

For any organization it is essential to have a common direction, and an understanding of why it is doing what they are doing. Our basic beliefs about how things work, and our attempts to figure them out, impact our response to those things. For example, someone who believes that poverty is the result of systemic injustice will work to change the political reality, whereas someone who believes that poverty is the result of personal choices will focus more on providing incentives to change a lifestyle. Similarly, our beliefs about eschatology (how the end times will play out) affect how we view world missions and our role in it. Those who believe that all nations must be reached in order for Christ to return are highly motivated in the areas of Scripture translation, for example.

This becomes especially important when we are approaching cross cultural issues. What are the basic beliefs of our culture as compared to the other culture? If we are starting from a place of believing that our culture is superior, our reactions to another culture will reflect this. At what level do we draw the line when it comes to crossing cultures? Is it at inviting someone into our own home, or visiting theirs? Is it allowing them to ride in our car, or participate in our small group? What about our children, and when they decide they want to date or marry someone from this culture?

Before beginning cross cultural ministry, or going any further if you are already in it, I would recommend a time of intentional introspection. What do you believe about the equality of all people? How does that play out on a spiritual level – is the American church inherently more sanctified than the foreign church? What connection is there, in your thinking at least, between physical poverty and spiritual poverty? Do you automatically assume that a poor person is necessarily a less mature Believer than you are, or an inherently worse human being? Are the way you dress, the norms of your culture, and the traditions of how you worship the end result of hundreds of years of a more spiritually advanced cultural heritage? And, just for fun, what color skin did Adam and Eve have?

When we go to another culture, we should always go as learners. I remember one of my dearest friends talking about the passage from Luke 13:34: "Jerusalem, Jerusalem…. How often I have longed to gather your children together, as a hen gathers her chicks under her wings, and you were not willing." He talked about how reading this in his native language conveys a deeper meaning. To me it is sort of a cute image, warm and fuzzy, rather than the fairly radical statement it actually is.

Picture an African village, with chickens running wild. It's dirty, dusty, and dangerous. Predators hover above, behind rocks, and in almost every bush. Storms rise up fast and strong, and there is no coop to hide in, so when trouble comes the chickies run to Momma Hen, who wraps her wings around them. She gives them not only a safe, warm, dry place to stay, but actually offers herself as a sacrifice, putting herself between the chicks and the potentially deadly danger. I did not get that image from those few words, but my friend did.

As believers we should also be seeking to grow our faith, and to deepen and strengthen our spiritual life. I have learned to pray at a deeper, more passionate level because of my interactions with believers raised in extreme poverty. I have been humbled at the literally unshakable faith in God's sovereignty of people who have experienced catastrophic natural disasters. After Hurricane Katrina hit the US Gulf Coast in 2005, I had the privilege of spending several months doing on-site coordination of volunteer relief efforts and working closely with the community as they struggled to get back on their feet. We spent endless hours pulling the ruined remnants of a lifetime of possessions from people's badly damaged and waterlogged homes, piling them on the street to be hauled away. Two signs I saw during my time there stand out in my memory. Both were hand- written on pieces of cardboard, and stuck to the front of debris piles containing the ruins of a family's earthly possessions. One read "This Sucks" and the other said "This pile of stuff was not our life, our life is hid in Christ."

CHAPTER 3

KEY SCRIPTURES

As you develop your own philosophy of cross cultural ministry or missions, don't forget to look to the Scriptures for guidance. Of course, it is dangerous to take a few passages out of context to create your approach to cross cultural connections, but there are some that offer great nuggets of wisdom.

"Though I am free and belong to no man, I make myself a slave to everyone, to win as many as possible. To the Jews I became like a Jew, to win the Jews. To those under the law I became like one under the law (though I myself am not under the law), so as to win those under the law. To those not having the law I became like one not having the law (though I am not free from God's law but am under Christ's law), so as to win those not having the law. To the weak I became weak, to win the weak. I have become all things to all men so that by all possible means I might save some."
(1 Cor. 9:19-21)

Paul in this passage is primarily talking about the law, and how we as Christians are both free from it and slaves to it, as John Piper discusses:

"In 1520 Martin Luther, the great Reformer in Germany, wrote a treatise called "The Freedom of the Christian." He began it with this paradox:

A Christian is a perfectly free lord of all, subject to none. A Christian is a perfectly dutiful servant of all, subject to all.

Then he explained:

These two theses seem to contradict each other . . . [But] both are Paul's own statements, who says in 1 Corinthians 9:19, "For though I am free from all men, I have made myself a slave to all," and in Romans 13:8, "Owe no one anything, except to love one another." Love, by its very nature, is ready to serve and be subject to him who is loved.

So Paul's strategy is love. It's exactly what he said in Galatians 5:13, "You were called to freedom, brethren; only do not turn your freedom into an opportunity for the flesh, but through love serve one another." Use your liberty to love by serving. That's what Paul says he is doing here in verse 19: "Though I am free from all *men*, I have made myself a slave [or servant] to all." That's what Paul—and Jesus—mean by love." [ii]

This verse resonates deeply with me, and I contextualize it for every situation in which I work. To the Kenyan I become like a Kenya, to the poor I become like the poor, etc. I will always be a white American, and that will never change, but I can go to great lengths to minister in a contextually appropriate manner. As a child I read the stories of Hudson Taylor, and how he was ridiculed and even ostracized for his radical approach to doing ministry in light of this verse. Amy Carmichael actually dyed her skin with coffee while ministering in India. Even today a missionary or international worker who dressed like a local would be subject to criticism and certainly a large dose of mockery.

We have often strayed to the opposite extreme, living like Americans wherever we go. We dress like we are in the States, we talk the same, watch the same TV, and strive to raise our children as if they are still back home. We surround ourselves with people like us, even creating whole industries to keep missionaries at the level they are accustomed to. Is this the call of the gospel? I am not arguing that we must live extraordinary lives in order to be considered faithful, as has become a trend of late. Anthony Bradley, in a *World* magazine article entitled "The New Radicalism" emphasizes this: "Today's millennial generation is being fed the message that if they don't do something extraordinary in this life they are wasting their gifts and potential." [iii]

Bradley makes a good general point, especially in light of 1 Thessalonians 4:11, which discusses the importance of living a quiet life, but I am talking specifically about those who are called to live and work in a cross cultural setting. The danger is in confusing our spiritual calling with our cultural identity. Our goal should not be to make the world England, as many missionaries in past centuries were told, but rather to show Christ to the world. What Paul is arguing in this passage is that we need to be willing to do whatever it takes to reach those from different cultures, not because we are cool hippy world-traveler types, but because we have a specific purpose. Piper says:

"Five times he (Paul) says that his aim is to win people. Verse 19: "that I might win the more." Verse 20: "

that I might win the Jews . . . that I might win those under the law." Verse 21: "That I might win those who are without law." Verse 22: "That I might win the weak."

So five times he says that his aim in adapting to the way people live is to win them. Then at the end of verse 22 in his summary statement he says, "I have become all things to all men, that I may by all means save some." So he says his aim differently here. Five times it was "to win" people; and now it is "to save" people." [iv]

Sometimes I think we forget that part of our purpose in life is to make disciples, and that we are called to the spread of the gospel. We can find a million excuses not to do things, such as the fear of not doing things the correct way, or causing more harm than good. To me, these verses give a way forward. I have become all things to all men so that by all possible means I might save some. It is a sacrificing of my cultural and personal identity with the specific goal of reaching others for Christ.

"And the LORD said to Joshua, "Today I will begin to exalt you in the eyes of all Israel, so they may know that I am with you as I was with Moses. Tell the priests who carry the Ark of the Covenant: 'When you reach the edge of the Jordan's waters, go and stand in the river.' " … Now then, choose twelve men from the tribes of Israel, one from each tribe. And as soon as the priests who carry the ark of the LORD -the Lord of all the earth—set foot in the Jordan, its waters flowing downstream will be cut off and stand up in a heap." So when the people broke camp to cross the Jordan, the priests carrying the Ark of the Covenant went ahead of them. Now the Jordan is at flood stage all during harvest.

Yet as soon as the priests who carried the ark reached the Jordan and their feet touched the water's edge, the water from upstream stopped flowing." (Joshua 3:7-15)

I love this passage. God used it tremendously in my life as a young man and a young believer, particularly in some of my first leadership roles. Joshua has been preparing for leadership for most of his life, and finally it is his turn. "I am with you, as I was with Moses," says God. This is true, but God does not work in the same way with Joshua that He does with Moses. With Moses, it is thunder and lightning, dramatic scenes, smiting the water, like something from a Hollywood movie. With Joshua, it is often hard work, strange requirements, and constant need to show his own faith. There is no smiting of the water here. Joshua's first big scene as a leader requires something that is borderline insanity: take the Ark of the Covenant (you know, the one that if you touch it the wrong way your face melts like in "Indiana Jones") and have the priests step into the river with it. Not just a regular river, which would have required faith enough, but the river at flood stage. I used to picture this as a docile scene, a large puddle, but now I have spent too much time around floods, and often seen the awesome destructive power of a flooded river. It roars and moves with incredible force. This is no pleasant step into a large puddle, but an act of radical faith, not an act to be performed by Joshua, but rather one that he has to convince the people to do.

There is always a struggle for Christians in deciding when to move and when to stay. Those on both sides of the argument point to various scriptures and spiritual principles to state their case. Generally the question is: do we stay and wait until God makes clear the time for movement or action, or do we continue to move and act until God tells us to stop? This story is a little bit of both, as the people have been waiting a long time to cross the Jordan, but it is also one of movement and action. The Scripture includes clear commands to go into all the world and make disciples, so we should not be making excuses about whether to act or not, but should rather be focusing on where and how we should go.

"Just as a body, though one, has many parts, but all its many parts form one body, so it is with Christ... Even so the body is not made up of one part but of many. Now if the foot should say, "Because I am not a hand, I do not belong to the body," it would not for that reason stop being part of the body. And if the ear should say, "Because I am not an eye, I do not belong to the body," it would not for that reason stop being part of the body. If the whole body were an eye, where would the sense of hearing be? If the whole body were an ear, where would the sense of smell be? But in fact God has placed the parts in the body, every one of them, just as he wanted them to be. If they were all one part, where would the body be? As it is, there are many parts, but one body. The eye cannot say to the hand, "I don't need you!" And the head cannot say to the feet, "I don't need you!" ...There should be no division in the body, but that its parts should have equal concern for each other. If one part suffers, every part suffers with it; if one part is honored, every part rejoices with it." 1 Corinthians 12: 12-16

This passage gives some great encouragement to the church about our dependence on each other, and the unity that should result from that. This is applicable in several practical ways, but it especially gives us a guideline about how we should treat each other, regardless of cultural or socio economic differences. Matthew Henry, in his Concise Commentary, sums up this passage:

"All the members of the body are useful and necessary to each other. Nor is there a member of the body of Christ, but may and ought to be useful to fellow-members. As in the natural body of man, the members should be closely united by the strongest bonds of love; the good of the whole should be the object of all. All Christians are dependent one upon another; each is to expect and receive help from the rest. Let us then have more of the spirit of union in our religion."

This verse will get more in depth discussion later, but it is important. Historically the Western churches had the Scriptures and were bringing them to places that did not have them. Places like still exist today, and perhaps some different rules apply. A vast majority of the work being done today in missions, ministry, and tent-making around the globe is happening where the local church already exists. We are one body, and we need each other. The American church needs the African church, and the African church needs the American church. A poor church needs a wealthy church, which perhaps is easy to see and agree with, but does that wealthy church need the poor church just as much? One church body cannot say to the other "I don't need you!" The church was not meant to be dependent, nor can it be independent: it needs to be interdependent.

"For I was hungry and you gave me food, I was thirsty

and you gave me drink, a stranger and you welcomed me, naked and you clothed me, ill and you cared for me, in prison and you visited me." Then the righteous will answer him and say, "Lord, when did we see you hungry and feed you, or see you thirsty and give you drink?". The king will say to them in reply, "Amen, I say to you, whatever you did to one of these least brothers of mine, you did for me." Matthew 25: 35-40

There are a number of passages calling us to be involved in mercy ministry. Isaiah 57 and Micah 6:8 could be used here as well. I chose this one because I read once that Mother Teresa based her entire ministry and life on this particular passage, saying: "Seeing and adoring the presence of Jesus, especially in the lowly appearance of bread, and in the distressing disguise of the poor." [v]

Let me be clear that I am not advocating the social gospel, nor I am I discussing salvation by works. We do not do good deeds as a way to earn salvation, but rather because we are saved we do good deeds. Faith without works is dead, a tree that bears no fruit is to be cursed and burned, and so on. The basic point here is that the church must be active in the world around it. Pastor Randy Nabors, Pastor Emeritus of New City Fellowship Chattanooga and founder of the New City Network, who has lived and preached cross cultural mercy ministry for more than forty years, sums it up this way: "The local church must be an agent of change in its own community." [vi]

Struggle with this; wrestle with it. The gospel calls us to sell everything we have, and give the money to the poor. It tells us that whatever we do to those in need, we are doing to Christ. These don't fit nicely into my personal doctrine box, nor into my ideas of how things should work. If I sell everything I have, obviously there is some room in there to keep some essential personal items, right? And then I give it to the poor, but does that mean I just walk up to the first random poor person I see and hand them a wad of cash, or should I carefully research charitable organizations to see which is doing the most good, without causing harm, and getting the biggest bang for the buck, or should I give this to the Deacons of my church to distribute among the widows and orphans, but only that belong to my own congregation? I keep getting these emails from a pastor in Nigeria…

We believe in the application of the whole scripture, not just taking one or two verses to make a point, but all of us have certain verses that resonate more strongly with us, or which God has used to teach us some specific thing. Those particular verses or themes have a strong influence on us, and particularly on how we act. There are many other verses that are applicable to this discussion, and that can be argued as being important influences on how we do ministry or missions cross culturally. I have just chosen a few as illustrations, though my own views and understanding are influenced by a great number of other passages and, I would like to claim, even by the entire Scriptures.

CHAPTER 4

PREACH, PRAY OR DIE

In some of my earliest missions training, we were told that missionaries must be prepared to preach, pray, or die at a moment's notice. It may seem cute and casual to say, but this was in an organization that had a long list of martyrs in its history, and some that had experienced things worse than being killed for their faith. I think there is importance in this mindset of being prepared, as 2 Timothy 4:2 says, in and out of season.

The team was working at a school in a slum area, and the indigenous school leader was very happy. Some of the team was doing physical labor, down on their hands and knees in the dirty clay, sweating profusely in the equatorial sun. Crowds were gathering at every window or doorway to watch these white foreigners work, and many were joking about how they didn't even know white people could sweat, because they had never seen them work hard before. This was too good of an opportunity to pass up, so the school leader called the team together, and opened the gates to the outside crowd, asking if they would like to hear from the visitors. She then turned to the team, and asked if someone would share a testimony. Silence. The awkward seconds turned into uncomfortable minutes, and no one responded. Maybe they were just tired. Included among the team were ministry leaders and teachers, people that should have easily been able to share a quick story or even a song, but the inhibitions were too strong. I stepped forward, but the school leader shook her head, the disappointment evident in her eyes, turned to the crowd, and began to tell them her own testimony.

Another time in a remote village church, a friend was asked to share, and he did, despite his fears. His testimony was being translated, and in his nervousness, he kept repeating, "Uhmmm," as he spoke. Every time he said this, the congregation roared back, "Amen." I can only imagine what they thought as they heard the translation, but he certainly kept their attention. On the streets in an American city, doing street-corner evangelism at lunchtime as part of missions training, we had to do a paint-board lesson. The man whose turn it was came from another country and language, and was both by culture and personality a reserved person. Professionally he had worked behind the scenes; he was not a "people person" at all. His voice was barely audible, and even if he could have been heard I don't think he would have been understood. He shook so much that the paint was all over the board, which didn't matter much because he stood in front of the board the entire time anyway. It was one of the worst presentations ever – he actually did everything wrong. But he did it, and as he continued and it got worse and worse, a strange thing happened. More and more people stopped, fascinated. What could be so important that this man would be willing to make such a miserable embarrassment of himself to tell it? We had more people stay after his presentation to talk with us than on any other day, certainly more so than the perfectly polished presentation I made.

Luke 12:11-12 tells us not to be anxious when we are called upon to give witness or defend our faith, because the Holy Spirit will at that time tell us what to say. When you are given the opportunity to share, take it! Stand up and speak the Scriptures that you know, and let the Spirit guide you. I once saw a young man, insecure and afraid of public speaking, stand up when given the opportunity to speak and deliver one of the most powerful sermons I have ever heard, and I have seen inner-city youth who only know a few words of Scripture stand up and share the little bit they know with great impact.

I find it incomprehensible when people do not take advantage of the opportunities given to them while on a trip or in a different cultural context. Isn't that the whole point, to be there and engage and share? Beyond this, though, it is utterly unbelievable to me when Christians refuse to pray. In fact, I test teams with this early on, asking for volunteers to pray, and when few hands go up, tell them that when they are given the opportunity to pray, every hand should go up. We should actually be always pushing for chances to pray. Often in the context of a closed country or culture, people will still ask to be prayed for, and why would we ever refuse that?

Trust in the Lord with all of your strength, lean not on your own understanding. Think of Moses, in Exodus 4:10-12. God tells him to go speak to Pharaoh, but Moses argues that he is not eloquent. Some speculate that Moses had a speech disorder, or perhaps after so many years away had lost much of his language skills. Whatever the case may be, Moses feels unable to proclaim God's truth, but God will not let him use that as an excuse. "Then the Lord said to him, "Who has made man's mouth? Who makes him mute, or deaf, or seeing, or blind? Is it not I, the Lord? Now therefore go, and I will be with your mouth and teach you what you shall speak." This is no excuse not to be prepared, but God will use your words to His glory if He is giving you the opportunity to share.

I would strongly encourage you to take a few minutes, even now, to jot out a testimony. We often think of a testimony as the story of how and when God called us, but a testimony is simply a good word, a story of something God has done in our life. Pick a passage that has particular meaning to you, and a brief story of how God used this in your life. It may be as simple as you feeling tired and God giving you strength to persevere, or as dramatic as a miracle or time when your physical life was in danger. Keep the focus on Christ, and not on yourself or on what the Devil did. Remember the purpose is to point people to Christ, to testify to who He is and what He has done. "Keep It Simple, Stupid."

Thankfully I have yet to be asked to die on a mission trip, though I have on numerous occasions had guns in my face or been in potentially deadly situations. To me, this is more a question of willingness to sacrifice. We do, arguably, sacrifice our time, money, and comfort level to go on a mission or disaster trip, but the question is how far we are willing to be inconvenienced for the Gospel. "Put to death therefore what is earthly in you: sexual immorality, impurity, passion, evil desire, and covetousness, which is idolatry" (Colossians 3:5). Are we willing to die this kind of death, for the greater sake of mission?

CHAPTER 5

INTERDEPENDENCE

My friend Dick Allen first introduced me to the term "interdependence" from, and he expounds upon it in his useful book, <u>The Genesis Principle of Leadership</u>. He is talking about leadership, but I think the basic tenet is the same, and applicable to cross cultural dynamics: "Remember, you are interdependent. You are totally and dynamically reliant upon God and your fellow human beings for you well-being and continued existence. Nonetheless, you remain irreducibly distinctive, independent, and irreplaceable with even greater individual capacity, influence, and significance, finding the center of your existence and significance in God and others." [vii]

Much has been said and written of late about avoiding the creation of dependency. I applaud this effort, though we do need to be careful to distinguish the uniqueness of the priority of the church, versus that of a professional development organization. Brian Fikkert and Steve Corbett have written a helpful book, <u>When Helping Hurts</u>, [viii] on avoiding dependency, specifically in community development, that I think most readers would find a thought-provoking and challenging discussion. The church is also not meant to be independent. By this I am not talking about the theology behind denominationalism, but rather a sense of being a part of the global body of Christ.

One of the reasons I love being a part of disaster response ministry is that I see this connectivity played out more clearly. Churches who have fought for years over shared parking lots, sheep stealing, and disputed calls in church league games ten years ago were able to put all that junk aside when disasters hit and actually help each other. The church (and we as believers, even as human beings) was not made to be alone, but to be part of a community: a global community. My wife adds this: "Many people equate asking for help with weakness, thus hindering themselves from serving where the Lord has opened a door. This is sad. 'I can do it all by myself' should be left at the toddler stage."

I Corinthians 12 talks about the body of Christ, and how we need each other. This means that we need others as much as they need us. We believe we are all sinners in need of grace, and we come from a heritage that celebrates the equality of all human beings, and yet we often fall into the trap of spiritually-based cultural elitism: we begin to act and talk as if the American church is superior to churches in lesser-developed areas. I call this spiritual racism, as I think it is very dangerous to the wellbeing of the church. We cannot continue to go about global work in a one-sided fashion, as if all the good is on our side and the bad on the other. I have seen foreigners walk to the front of a church, take a microphone from the local music leader, and announce that they are going to sing a song. Try that in most American churches and you would end up on the floor with a bloody nose. Visiting missionaries or mission teams may tell local pastors that they are going to do this or that, or even preach the sermon.

We also believe in the authority of the local church, and must function under its authority, when possible. When we go into areas where the local church exists, we go to serve it, not to rule over it, and not necessarily as equal partners. Historically it was different, and to some extent, as I mentioned previously, there are some differences when there is no legitimate local church. I applaud the idea of coming alongside as a partner, but that implies equality – on both sides. A missionary who has never actually been involved in a church plant back home is not an equal partner to the African pastor who has been planting churches for twenty years. A stay-at-home mom who goes on a short-term trip has no business telling the elderly school director how to run the school.

Not only does partnership necessitate an equality of skill and experience, but it requires a recognition of the equality of all human beings. Elitism and paternalism negate partnership, and too often this is what is meant when we talk of partnership: "I, who am better educated and come from what I believe to be a vastly superior church and national culture, will lower myself to come alongside you - a poor, ignorant and probably theologically weaker younger brother - as an equal partner, by which I mean that I will tell you what to do and point out all that you are doing wrong, and to which you will listen because let's face it, I single handedly control the flow of external funding that you need to run your church." I am getting snarky, but this is a subject that frustrates me, and that I feel that it is getting worse and not better. We forget that we are not the source of our existence or resources, and in reality we should be thankful that the Lord is working through us – and them.

I mentioned the dependence of the foreign church on international funds, and I recognize that this is a substantial problem. The western or wealthier church is essentially buying the right to influence the church leadership, and the financially-challenged local pastor sees no other option. He might be reaping the benefits in that he can move his family to a safer place, send his kids to a better school and maybe even a foreign university, and drive a car that actually runs. Interdependence breaks down a little at this level, and though I can talk all day about how essential interdependence is on a spiritual, intellectual, and cultural level, I admit that the answers on the financial side may be a bit more difficult. In other words a poor church, particularly in an economically-depressed location, is often very much dependent on a wealthier church, and there is little reciprocity. An American missionary serving in a developing country is another example of this conundrum, though you could make the argument that they use the needs of their destination as a means to raise the support that enables them to live at the level they do.

CHAPTER 6

HOW THEN SHOULD WE GO?

To borrow from Francis Schaeffer's famous question, "How then should we live?,"[ix] I ask the question, "How then should we go?" I hope I have convinced you by now that we need to think differently about the way we approach cross-cultural work, and that there is, perhaps, a better way to do that, but what does that look like? This necessitates a look at what is, and suggestions for how we can modify our approach going forward.

Jim Raymo, in his book <u>Marching to a Different Drummer</u>, conducts an excellent discussion on the issue of missionary affluence. This is an area that I, and others of my generation, have struggled with. In serving as the Chairman of my church's Missions Committee, I too have seen requests for missions support that are astonishingly high, and in my travels have seen missionaries living at an extreme level. One missionary had at least seven servants, and justified this by saying it was their way of helping the local economy. Raymo looks at some of the arguments supporting missionary affluence, and this stood out:

"A missionary from another agency says locals have a concept of what the Western person is like, and to gain their respect, expectations must be met by building a better house, owning a better vehicle, etc. Too close an identification with native culture can diminish standing in the community and, therefore, the credibility of the message being preached."[x]

As I struggled through this, not always understanding the complexities, I developed a simple scale that helped me keep things in perspective. On the one hand I look at the level of ministry, and on the other the level of living. If the level of ministry is equal to or above the level of living, then I accept that. If, however, the level of living is higher than the level of ministry, then there is an issue, and the bigger this gap the bigger the issue. "Too close an identification with native culture" is a concept we have heard missionaries defend, and it sends a message to the local believers that I am here to know you, but I build a wall so that you won't know me. This equals no relationship.

This can be argued both ways, and I understand that. Though we are all called to sacrificial living, it is not fair to deny missionaries a comfortable lifestyle, which in many international settings might look like more than it is. Support levels and perceived affluence are things that must be worked out in consultation with the local church or community leadership. Too often these policies and amounts are set by U.S. based headquarters, who pull large percentages out of received funds for their own administrative empires. Often the lifestyle level is influenced by the existing veteran missionary community, some of whom have grown accustomed to lives of luxury and do not want to be made to look bad by the new radical missionary. An African pastor told me a story of an elderly missionary who lives in a nice part of the city, and has a permanent tee time at the best golf course in town, six days a week. On Sundays he gets up early and is driven out to the village where he planted a successful church many decades before. He spends the day there, and returns to his own bed, disconnected from the very people he is there to serve.

The beauty of my simple scale is that it allows for better living if the ministry is there. I have met people who live in massive homes, drive nice cars, and even hire servants, but have an incredible ministry. Some of these people use their affluence to increase their ministry, while others see it as a necessary retreat from the intense work they do in the daytime. This is often the case for those work in slum areas. They will be in the slum, covered in filth and human tragedy from early in the morning until late in the day, but then return to a hot bath, safe night's sleep, and awake refreshed and renewed for another day of battle. I applaud this, so please do not think I am saying that all missionaries must live in little mud huts and starve their own children for the sake of the Gospel.

My argument is that if we are truly seeking to follow the example of Christ, who came to earth as a child, fully human, we need to consider closely how our lifestyle, or the perception of our lifestyle, might be impacting our ministry.

In returning to a country frequently, I got to know a van driver well, and often asked his opinion on things and had some great conversations with him (one of my favorite pictures is of him and me standing deep in conversation, with monkeys on our heads). We sat in the van one day at a popular shopping area, waiting for some team members who had run in for coffee. A van pulled in next to us, with big lettering declaring itself as a missions van, and the white people inside piled out of the back. The last one out left the door wide open, and as the driver came around the front he saw my friend and made a face, obviously directed at the recent occupants of his van. He did not see me. I asked my friend, then and there, "What is your general impression of foreign white missionaries?" He deliberated, and then moved so he was looking me directly in the eye. "I think, that in the Scriptures, it says it best. If a man does not work, a man does not eat."

A number of years ago I found myself in the conference room of a seminary doing their missions conference. Present in the room were missions professors, American pastors, foreign pastors, and ministry leaders. Everyone was killing time, so I took advantage of the situation to ask a simple question: "How should we, as Americans, do missions today?" Several full whiteboards later, the group came to a consensus. We go with boldness and humility. We have boldness because of the confidence that the gospel is true, that God is who He says He is, and that ultimately He is in control. We have the truth. We also have a degree of confidence in knowing that we come from a country that allows great opportunity, and that simply being American might open certain doors (something that can easily be misused). I experienced this when I got lost in the Kibera slum one day, and accidently walked into the wrong school. I was a total stranger, but the teacher immediately stopped class and invited me to the front to share with the students.

We also must go with Humility. We are not inherently better, smarter, or more spiritual than anyone else; we are just as broken and dependent upon God's grace and mercy. Beyond that, our heritage is as ugly as any other out there: slavery, genocide, oppression, arrogance, and corruption. We live in a country that has major problems with crime, poverty, abuse, and substance use. Micah 6:8 sums it up well: "He has told you, O man, what is good; and what does the Lord require of you but to do justice, and to love kindness, and to walk humbly with your God?"

CHAPTER 7

BE RELATIONAL

I heard a missionary speak recently, and he began his story by talking about his best friend in Spain, who was a local Spaniard. Such a simple thing, but it really blessed my heart to hear. The heart of the gospel is relational. It is one-on-one, intimate, and genuine. Our call is to go into all the world and develop intimate connections for the purpose of teaching or training (make disciples). The word became flesh and dwelt among us (John 1:14): God himself became man and walked among us. He could have been born in the mightiest palace, or come down with an army of angels and chariots of fire. He could have declared Himself to the whole earth in some magnificent way, but instead He came as one of us, a simple common man, walking this dusty broken ground. "He walks with me and He talks with me, Along life's narrow way…" [xi]

Many organizations place an emphasis on relational ministry, and have great catch phrases:
"Earn the right to speak"; "People don't care how much you know until they know how much you care." These are good reminders, but let's take them even further. Earning the right to speak is good, but let's earn the right to hear and to be heard, and the right to laugh, and the right to cry or be cried on. It should be

reciprocal, though we are often afraid of reciprocal relationships because we are afraid we will be viewed as being weak. I think when we know each other's weaknesses and bear with one another we learn to love each other more. Love is weakness. Christ's strength is made perfect in us, and we are given more room to love.

Build lasting friendships. I believe the test of a good mission trip is whether true friendships were begun, and how long they last. I have people I consider to be some of my dearest friends that I met on mission trips more than twenty years ago, and though I have not seem some since, I know the connection is still there. In 2006 I went on a trip to Kenya to meet with local church leaders and missionaries to see how my church in the U.S. could better connect with them, and on that trip met a young Kenyan lady, the worship leader in her church, who quickly became my best friend, and then my wife. One of the things she tells people preparing to go overseas is, "Seek to know, to find out about people."

A good litmus test will be to keep an eye on who your friends are. Let the people you are there to serve become your close friends, even if that takes more effort. Real friends not only invite each other into their homes, but show up unannounced. Real friends call for both good and bad things, and are called back in return. Real friends speak the truth, and are still loved for it.

Do not just fraternize with fellow Americans or missionaries, or those few locals you view as equal. Make real local friends. If this is too much of a struggle, then perhaps this is not the ministry you are called to. Kevin Smith, Senior Pastor at New City Chattanooga, recently stated: "Don't go to Africa if you don't like black people in your own community."[xii]

The biblical scholar is now jumping up and down in his seat, waving his hand. What about Jonah? He hated the people God sent him to. He tried to run away and God physically and dramatically intervened, forcing Jonah to go to Ninevah. Despite his horrible attitude, God saved the city, and Jonah was furious at God for doing that. This is important, I believe in the Sovereignty of God, and know that he works in His own ways to accomplish His purposes on earth and in our lives. We are all broken, we are all sinners, and God uses us for His glory. Knowing ourselves will always take us back to the cross. We need our Redeemer every day. I am not saying that a lack of cultural sensitivity or awareness in ministry prohibits God from doing His work, but am instead calling us all to be aware of our own sins, both personal and cultural, and to follow Paul's exhortation to make ourselves slaves. Remember 1 Corinthians 9 tells us this is all for a purpose: to win as many as possible, to save some.

CHAPTER 8

THE WORDS OF MY MOUTH...

In the days when I travelled frequently, and while I was a teacher, I began every day by praying Psalm 19:14: "May the words of my mouth, and the meditations of my heart be acceptable in Your sight, O Lord my rock and my redeemer." I think also of Psalm 73:15: "If I had spoken out like that, I would have betrayed your children." When I am giving a talk on this subject, I usually break out into "Oh be careful little mouth what you say" at this point. Be glad you can't hear how badly I sing. Assume that everything you say will be overheard, and protect yourself from falling into the trap of gossip and bad mouthing the local people. Think carefully about how your words might sound, and be careful to avoid phrasing things to set yourself apart ("these people"). I sat once with a team in Africa and heard several team members start talking about "these people" and how dirty they were, and so on. As I glanced around at the team I caught the eye of the only African American on the team, an elderly lady, and I saw tears falling down her cheeks. I spoke to her later, and she said, "These people are me, Brian; that was me they were talking about. I've never been so mad, and embarrassed. It just hurts."

On several occasions I have overheard people talking

about me, and it was painful. I also remember sitting in a car in South America and listening to the missionary vent about the local people he worked with. When he exited the car I stayed behind, and softly asked the local driver if he had understood. He looked at me and nodded, and I simply put my hand on his shoulder and apologized.

This goes both ways. Our unintentional praise can radically change a person's day, and bring great strength and encouragement in a difficult time. Imagine if you were sitting in your office, and overheard your coworkers talking about how great you were, what a blessing it was to be around you, and what a witness you were for the gospel. Imagine how you would feel!

This also goes beyond personal. In responding to the tsunami in Sri Lanka, we were under strict admonishment not to proselytize, and armed Buddhist soldiers accompanied us everywhere to ensure that we complied. After a few days, though, we noticed that the residents of the resettlement camp would gather around us while we sat and ate our lunch, while the soldiers stayed closer to the road. Local church members were always with us, and were bilingual. We began doing devotions at lunch, and the church members would translate. We sat in a circle, but the residents could clearly hear us. I will never forget the tears in one man's eyes, a church member who was with us almost every day, as he later sat with some of the refugee children and explained the gospel to them.

On another occasion I was in the home of a dear brother who had been raised as a radical Muslim, but converted to Christianity by reading the Koran. There are several mentions of the name "Issa" When he asked what those were in reference to, an Islamic scholar told him they were in reference to the Christian Jesus, and that he could read the Bible to find out more about Him. He did that, and discovered Jesus claiming to be the first, the last, and the only. This led to him becoming a follower of the true God. Many of his family members were not Christians, and one young man was staying in his home, and sitting on the coach while he and I ate lunch at the table. He could hear every word we said, and we tested that by making a few jokes. He chuckled, but still tried to pretend he was not paying attention. My friend then began asking me intentional questions about my faith, my testimony, and the Scripture. He knew exactly what to ask and what not to ask, and for almost an hour we shared the gospel with this young man. He never pretended to listen, but we know he heard. He made no confession of Christ, but we know that the Word of God is living and active, and does not return void.

Everyone who travels collects things, and I like to collect testimonies. I love to hear how Christ brought people to Himself, what random events, people, or situations were used. It pushes me to be more intentional in speaking out my faith, in singing Christian songs in public, or praying out loud at a restaurant. So often it is a casual passing event that triggers the avalanche: a young man walking through a mall and having a random stranger tell him that Jesus loves him; a student debating religion with her siblings, and challenged to read the Bible simply to win an argument.

The Word of God is living and active, and we must live like we believe that. Our careless derogatory words about a culture or people group can cause great harm, but a simple loving response can change lives.

CHAPTER 9

ASKING OR CRITICIZING?

What are your questions actually saying? Are you using questions to criticize? As I was preparing to walk out of the house the other day, my wife asked me, "Is that what you are wearing today?" She obviously knew that it was what I was wearing, and so her question was an attempt to draw attention to something she did not like or approve of; in this case the way I was dressed. Her question was actually a thinly-veiled criticism, and an effective way to get me to change my clothes. It is good to ask genuine, honest questions, and it will help you learn about the culture and understand things that are different or make you uncomfortable. Be careful, however, that you are not hiding a criticism or trying to make a suggestion.

The school was deep in a slum area, and too many children were crammed into the small building. It was hot, and smelly, and uncomfortable for the visitors. The school head was proud of the building, and the work that had been done on it, and of the kids. She reminded me very much of a mother hen. The team member was frustrated, and had been muttering under her breath for some time about the small size, the smell, and the heat. I think she was trying to find an indirect way to tell the school head that it was an unhealthy environment, so she said they should tell an American mission team to come fix the building. I can't remember her exact words, but her words and her tone conveyed judgment and condemnation on the existing building, and I could see the school head deflate. I was frustrated. Here we were to encourage and support this dear lady in her ministry, and instead we ended up demeaning her work. It's a bit out of context, perhaps, but it makes me think of Acts 10:15: "Do not call unclean that which God has made clean."

One of the things I have been blessed by is getting to put some of these lessons into practice, as we use what we have learned to train people before they travel. I have seen people strengthened in their faith, have seen them be an encouragement to the local church, and have learned quite a bit myself from watching them intentionally pursue better connections in their interactions. I travelled with an older man who was full of wonder at being in Africa. This was more than he had ever dared to dream, to be in Africa. He made lots of cultural mistakes, some rather humorous and some quite embarrassing, but his overall sense of joy was contagious. He also asked tons of questions, often about the most minute or trivial of things. Why do the cows have different shaped horns? Why are the houses painted this color or that? And on and on. His questions, though, were transparently genuine, heartfelt. People were happy to try to answer, and when he left he was remembered fondly in the local community, and asked to return again and again.

"Not all who wander are lost."[xiii] It is good to wonder as we wander. A great way to build connections is through asking questions, and often the local people will thoroughly enjoy that time. As I pursued my wife, and as we progress in our marriage, I have spent many happy hours answering questions from her family about me, about my home, my family, my culture. I do not take offense at this, but rather welcome it as a way for us all to know each other better, and for our connection to be strengthened.

CHAPTER 10

SEEING OR JUDGING?

A picture I use in training of Haiti after the earthquake was taken in a remote village in the mountains. A young Haitian girl is pictured walking up the hill in the midst of some rubble, alongside her grandfather, and carrying food to our team. After studying the picture, folks notice that she is wearing soccer cleats with her school uniform, and I ask what thoughts this triggers. Generally the response is that those were probably the only shoes she had to wear, and there is a sadness that moves people to think about bringing shoes for poor children who have to wear cleats to school. But wait: my four-year-old daughter has worn her soccer cleats to the grocery store, and often wears all kinds of crazy goofy clothing: socks that don't match, multiple layers of clothing, and whatever shoes she currently loves. Today it is pink cowgirl (not cowboy!) boots. What if this Haitian girl is wearing soccer cleats just because she wants to, or maybe it is because she had to climb up the hill to bring us food and so her Grandfather made her put them on? In truth, she owns multiple pairs of shoes.

It is good and important to see and be aware of the things around you, particularly things that may seem different. Different is not necessarily wrong. A fun quiz I often use with training teams involves asking about things that seem wrong to us, but are correct in their culture or context (the word rubbers, for instance). I tell the story of when I was meeting with my wife's family to discuss marriage arrangements, a complicated procedure in many African cultures, but necessary to establish the legitimacy of the marriage in the eyes of the community, especially as we intend to have a long term connection and ministry. As we sat around tea carrying out the requisite greetings and small talk, an uncle of hers suggested that we table the discussion on the marriage. I protested strongly, stating that we were all there at that time, and there was not much time until the wedding, and that we needed to talk right then. There were strange glances in my direction, but as I felt already miles outside my comfort zone, I did not understand. A year later, I read in the local paper that the Parliament had tabled a discussion and then voted to pass the issue. A sinking feeling swept over me, so I asked the Pastor I was staying with what "tabled" meant. He looked at me like I was a child: "Tabled, as in to put on the table, or to discuss immediately." I could do nothing but laugh, realizing how much of an idiot I must have sounded, for in my culture, "tabled" means to take off the table and wait for a future time.

"We instinctively tend to limit for whom we exert ourselves. We do it for people like us, and for people whom we like. Jesus will have none of that. By depicting a Samaritan helping a Jew, Jesus could not have found a more forceful way to say that anyone at all in need - regardless of race, politics, class, and religion - is your neighbour. Not everyone is your brother or sister in faith, but everyone is your neighbour, and you must love your neighbour." (Tim Keller) [xiv]

When the disciples return to where Jesus was waiting (John 4:27), they marvel to find Him talking to the Samaritan woman, but the Scripture is careful to point out that though they could have asked what was happening, they did not. They saw that something different and unusual was happening, which was probably a common experience for them as they walked around with Jesus, but they withheld their judgment, and obviously later heard the full story of what had transpired.

Romans 14:8 states: "Why do you pass judgment on your brother? Or you, why do you despise your brother? For we will all stand before the judgment seat of God." Avoid rushing to judgment, lest you be judged. Bite your tongue, hold off until you can get more information, and actually learn what is really happening. I'm as guilty of this as the next, but so often we see one side or a small portion of something, and assume we know what is actually happening. Also remember that people are seeing you, and may be making judgments based on your actions.

As you see things that are clearly different, or wrong to you, stop and think. Check your tendency to think that you know better. Ask a friend from the culture if there is something you are missing, or misunderstanding. Do some research. It's possible you may not ever understand, or it may actually be something inappropriate that you may need to follow up on later, in the appropriate manner.

In a quiz I have given to teams, I ask for people to

answer this question: Americans drive on the right side of the road, and many other countries drive on which side? The correct answer is of course the left side, but so often we answer with "the wrong side."

CHAPTER 10A

PRACTICAL IMPLICATIONS OF SEEING OR JUDGING: HOUSING

I looked out of the window of the guest room, and all I could see were walls and barbed wire. The tops of the walls were covered in sharp shards of broken Coke bottles, and a security guard stood outside the massive gate. I went downstairs to a lovely home, full of foreigners, without a single local person inside. This has happened to me too many times to count, and though I understand the need for safety, it makes me feel isolated and uncomfortable.

The discussion earlier about affluent living touches on this, but it is worth revisiting. Often while travelling this is beyond our control, and we have to live under the rules of the house or community we are staying in, but if you find yourself in a housing situation that is detrimental to your work, ministry, or building of cross-cultural connections, be loving and creative in finding ways to make it work. A favorite trick of mine was to ask my hosts if I could invite a friend over for dinner, and then bring a local (often to their surprise). If I thought this would offend or be too much, I might invite my hosts out for a dinner, and include numerous local friends in the dinner party. My parents came to visit me while I was working in South Africa, and my mother in particular was frustrated by the obvious divisions between races, and how the wealthy white ministry leaders treated the poor black local workers. She devised a plan to host a large barbecue, with lots of meat, and invite both parties to come and eat together, and then made a big show of us doing all the cleanup ourselves.

While safety concerns sometimes make such things necessary, try to avoid a substantial gap between the level of which you are living and that of the people with whom you are working. Living as close as possible to the community you are trying to connect with will greatly increase the opportunities you have for ministry, and the impact you will have on the local people. Also let your house be accessible and invite people over (and not just the ones that look like you!). I have often heard from local believers that they have never been invited into the home of a white missionary or foreigner for personal social reasons, even though they have invited those people into their homes. I have also heard a story of a missionary family more than thirty years ago who lived in a certain low-income community. Thirty years later the local people still talked about how they lived, how their doors were always open, and how the neighborhood kids basically lived in their home. They hired security guards because they were told they had to, but the security guards felt so at home they invited their friends, and set up a little village in the back yard – and these missionaries loved it. Their kids went to local schools, they worked hard to try to learn the language, and their love for the people was evident. This should be the norm, not the exception. It was very much how I was raised in my small hometown in upstate New York, and it is how we try to run our home now, even with small children. I tell visitors that after the third time they come, we will teach them how to break into our house so they can come anytime, even if we are not around.

I have previously mentioned John 1:14: "The Word became flesh and dwelt among us." Think about how radical Jesus' life was. Not only did He come down as a baby into all our mess, but He chose a very normal upbringing and social class for His human life. He could have been born in the mightiest palace and still completed the work of the cross, but He wanted to be among us, one of us, to walk in our shoes and feel our pain.

CHAPTER 10B

PRACTICAL IMPLICATIONS OF SEEING OR JUDGING: TRANSPORT

In Sri Lanka after the tsunami, a group of us young men had some free time in the capital city, and decided to ride the three-wheel motorcycle carts, or trishaws. We ended up in several different ones, and as we pulled out, one of the guys reached out and slapped the side of the other trishaw. "Tag!" he yelled, and the game was on. In and out of traffic, through big streets and small our drivers raced, with one of us hanging out trying to smack the other trishaw, back and forth. It was great fun, and no harm was done. The drivers were having as much fun as us, and were paid well for the adventure. I shudder to think of this happening with some of the teams I have led, and all the horrible things that could have happened. Too often my lessons were learned the hard way, through mistakes made by me or the teams I was with, and it was only God's grace that protected us, but that is not an excuse to be stupid. Do not put the Lord your God to the test.

It is interesting that transportation can be one of the most traumatic experiences for foreigners, whether here in the U.S. or overseas. Frequently I hear first-time travelers talk about how horrible the driving was, and someone else will chime in that it could not have been nearly as bad as what they experienced in some other place. For Americans overseas it is often the chaos and closeness of the traffic that is disturbing, coupled with the creativity of drivers and the unusual obstacles encountered. My personal favorite was a camel versus bus accident. For foreigners coming to the U.S. it is the speed of our interstates and the rapid changing of lanes, entering and exiting roads, as well as the bizarre way people actually follow the rules most of the time. A driver in the middle of the night with no other cars in sight will generally still stop at a stop sign or red light.

I have spent many hours riding public transportation overseas, and yet hardly ever do in my own hometown. Often it is a very social experience, crammed into spaces meant for someone half my size and with at least five more people in the vehicle than it is meant to carry. It can be a great time to do casual outreach, speaking to other team members or local friends about your faith, knowing full well that everyone else in the vehicle is trying hard to listen to everything you say, and it can be a fun and inexpensive way to see parts of a region you would never go to otherwise. It's usually good for your prayer life, as you will likely have multiple near-death experiences, and that's just in the first few miles. I have had to get out and push buses through chest deep flash floods, have been proposed to many times, have had total strangers sit on my lap for substantial periods of time, and once accidently hijacked a BMW. The actual act of travel can be a fairly significant part of ones experience.

Again there are safety concerns, and your organization may have policies that restrict you, but remember your vehicle is a part of your ministry as well. Try to use local transport sometimes, or walk when possible. If you are able, give rides to people and don't be afraid to stop and pick up people you know who are walking down the road. Keep in mind what your level of living will look like to the people you work with, and consider buying a car that is not top-of-the-line.

I love walking in different countries. While travelling alone, I liked to get out of the airports and just walk around during my layovers. You can smell culture, and feel it; the unique weather, the way the sun lights up the cities, the looks on people's faces as they walk. In some places people smile randomly; in others a smile only comes in response to a smile. Some cultures make eye contact, while others work hard to avoid it. I have had some of the greatest and most random conversations just wandering around, like the time I met Jimmy, who told me that he is the other son of God, Jesus' brother, but messed up and now he can't get back to heaven. We talked for a good hour as we walked into town, and then he asked me for money and I politely said no, and we went our separate ways.

On a more practical note, be wise. I have been robbed on public transport and have had teams robbed while walking. I have ended up lost and in dangerous situations far too many times. If you do get lost, don't panic. Go into a store and ask employees for help, or look for school students travelling in a pack. I fell asleep once on public transport, and woke after dark in a place I did not recognize. I immediately exited the vehicle, and began walking at a normal place towards some lights in the distance. I saw an elderly man walking alone, and moved close to him, matching his pace. After some time, I saw a group of students exiting a school, and moved into their group. One of them moved near to me, and asked where I needed to go. I told her, and she quickly whispered directions and bus instructions. I made it home, tired, safe, and hopefully a little wiser. This is when good cross-cultural skills come in handy, and you can make quick connections with people that can help you safely home.

CHAPTER 10C

PRACTICAL IMPLICATIONS OF SEEING OR JUDGING: FOOD

In the first few years of our cross-cultural marriage, we fought more about food than anything else. What we ate, when we would eat, how much we ate or threw away, and who we ate with were all things that could cause conflict. Often in cross-cultural settings this can be one of the biggest areas of stress. Is it more polite to eat everything in front of you and get sick, or to politely refuse and risk offending your host? What is safe and what is not? To me, one of the worst parts is that in each place I travel to I discover some incredible food or meal, and then have to leave knowing I will likely crave it the rest of my life and never get to eat it again. The first time you eat a ripe mango straight from the tree in some remote village, you will understand.

I have also been incredibly sick from things I ate or drank, and have seen trips ruined because of this. I strongly encourage you to educate yourself on what is safe to eat and drink, and what needs to be avoided. I have also seen people be incredibly rude to hosts because they do not like the food being served. There is a wise path, which is to speak honestly. If you invited me to your home, and served something I do not like or cannot eat, I would simply inform you of that in a polite manner, and you would likely offer me something else, or excuse me from eating - and possibly mock me after I left - but no dramatic scene or great offense would take place. I would not act as if I were eating the worst thing ever, with groaning and horrendous facial expressions, and most likely I would not try to pretend to eat while instead sliding the food to the dog, or throwing it over the rocks to the monkeys.

Generally you eat in private, and can eat whatever you want. If you are inviting people to your home you want to be considerate and aware of local norms, but basically you can cook what you like. I always encourage short-term visitors to bring snacks from home, like trail mix, so that they know they can always eat something later that will at least carry them through. This is not always an option. Anthony Bourdain used to host a show called "No Reservations," in which he travels to a wide variety of locations and samples whatever it is the locals eat. In a memorable episode he visits Namibia, and eats food that is particularly vile. He does his best to eat it, knowing full well he will get sick. Though there is much he says and does I do not agree with, I think we can learn from how he interacts with different cultures, again remembering 1 Corinthians 9 and that we have a different goal: to win a few.

If you are invited to a local home, or out to a local restaurant, use common sense (and carry some Pepto-Bismol). Eat what you can, don't be afraid to try new things, but be polite. Explain to your host that your stomach is sensitive, and you are not used to the food, thus shifting the negative onto yourself. Claim jetlag, that mysterious ailment that conveniently gets travelers out of many undesired things. A friend had travelled up to a remote village to visit with the tribal leaders. He was not feeling well from the long bumpy journey, and had some stomach issues from too much spicy food the preceding days. The villagers had made a large meal to welcome his group, and he gently and lovingly explained that his stomach was weak and he could not eat the food, but that he was very appreciative. He sat under a tree to rest, and a bit later the villagers came back with a second meal that they had prepared just for him. He had no choice then but to eat, and was glad for the Pepto-Bismol.

Another friend of mine tells the story of an old revered female missionary in Asia. While visiting a church, she was served fish eyes. The visitors waited expectantly to see this prim and proper lady pop an eyeball in her mouth. Instead she help up the plate, and said a prayer of blessing. After the prayer she reminded them of the story of Jesus serving the disciples, and how the first shall be last. She told the church members that they had honored her by serving her first, but she would honor them by serving the food to them. By the time the plate got back to her, the eyeballs were gone, and no one was paying much attention to her anymore.

When you are out with locals and stop for food, always be prepared to pay for their food – otherwise don't stop. I see this too often, where a team will want to buy food, often the same junk food they can get at home, but will not offer to buy for the local church member, driver, or translator with them, leaving this person in an awkward position, as they may not be able to afford the food. Don't be surprised or offended if they refuse, or simply order the "boring" local food they eat every day,

as this may be way outside their own cultural experience.
I remember taking a team to a fancy and expensive
restaurant at the end of a trip. As was our custom, we
invited a number of the local church folks and ministry
leaders to come with us. Things got a little out of control
and we ended up with a large crowd and a huge bill, but
what I most remember is that though we were eating a
buffet style meal, several of the older local men only ate
their traditional food, which I could have purchased a
month's worth of for the amount I paid for their buffet
meals. The next time around we decided to ask church
members to cater for us, so they benefited financially and
the team still got a special meal with friends.

Take your lead from the locals, watch what and how
they eat, and let your eating be an experience that
enhances your connection. I remember eating with some
local friends in Ethiopia, a large communal bread bowl,
and the girl next to me rolled up a big handful of bread
and meat and shoved it into my mouth. I was single at
the time, and briefly wondered if this was some weird
mating ritual, and if I had accidently just gotten married,
but then I noticed the others at the table were doing
likewise. It was a bonding experience.

CHAPTER 10D

PRACTICAL IMPLICATIONS OF SEEING OR JUDGING: CLOTHES

In the 1800's, Hudson Taylor was considered a madman for dressing in traditional clothing to try to reach the Chinese more effectively. Today, in many parts of the world, there is an actual style of dressing called "missionary." It generally involves khaki shorts, hiking boots, baggy shirts with pockets, and some sort of floppy hat. This represents no indigenous culture in the world, but rather seems to be some sort of tribute to British colonialism. Having been a history teacher, I could launch into a long monologue here about the sun setting on the British Empire, but will rather simplify it to say that being perceived to glorify colonialism is not likely to help develop strong cross- cultural connections (probably not even in England).

How you dress can say a great deal about how you respect the people you are among. Take the lead from local church or community leaders in how you should be dressing. If they are wearing long pants, you shouldn't be wearing shorts. If they wear shirt and tie to church, don't show up in an old t-shirt. If you are in a leadership position, this becomes even more important. Many cultures expect the leader or speaker to dress in a suit. This is not the time to make a statement about your freedom in Christ, and how He loves us no matter what we wear, and that you want to be welcoming of everyone no matter what they wear.

Realize that local people may consider things appropriate that you would question, or may simply be wearing what they have access to. I have seen women wearing shirts with highly inappropriate comments on them, even in church. I generally assume that they do not know what the saying means, and there is nothing gained by brining attention to it.

For many years I wore shorts while travelling in Africa, as I saw many other missionaries doing so. After marrying a Kenyan, my loving and ever-observant spouse asked me if I saw many other men wearing shorts. I said yes, and received a funny look in response. "African men, she qualified, "not missionaries." I thought for a moment, and realized I did not generally see African men in shorts, and certainly not at church or other formal settings. She proceeded to explain to me that under colonial rule, many African adult men were forced to wear khaki shorts, like school boys, as a reminder that they were children to their colonizers. Missionaries adopted this look because they too saw Africans as children, but in more of a spiritual sense. Suffice it to say that I am far more careful about when I wear shorts in Africa.

CHAPTER 10E

PRACTICAL IMPLICATIONS OF SEEING OR JUDGING: LANGUAGE

I sat at a popular roadside restaurant with my younger in-laws, who were mostly in their teens and young twenties. The old couple at the table next to us had obviously just finished a mission trip, and the husband was giving a farewell speech to several adult Africans seated with him. He spoke very loud, and extremely slow, as if speaking to babies. One of my sisters-in-law began to imitate him, and our whole table began to giggle uncontrollably.

The way you address people is important, and can communicate much about whether you respect them or not. Find and follow the local norms of who and how to talk to, particularly across age and gender lines. In some cultures men should not directly address women, for instance. I am prone to casual speech, but am careful to use proper titles when publically addressing older authority figures.

Learning at least a rudimentary amount of the local language is particularly helpful, and shows a willingness to step out of your comfort zone. Everyone who has ever tried to use a foreign language has made some humorous errors, such as ordering mud for lunch. Misuse of the language can cause problems or embarrassment.

I heard a young development worker describing his work to a panel of international donors, and in trying to impress them, he claimed that the locals had given him an African name, as if this were a sign that he had been successful in crossing into another culture. He spoke at some length about how everywhere he went people knew his African name, and how this showed how successful his work was. Most of the panel nodded as if quite impressed, but one man, an older gentleman who looked like he had spent some years under tropical suns, leaned back a little in his chair with a questioning look on his face. When the young man finished, he asked if he would mind telling them what his African name was. "Mzungu!" he replied. I am not sure how the gentleman held back his laughter, for Mzungu means "white person" and is liberally thrown in the direction of any foreigner, hundreds of times a day.

When the person you are speaking to knows little to no English, do not revert to baby talk (loud and slow). Yes, slow down, and use simpler language, but be careful your tone is not condescending. When I was on a trip with a young man from an inner-city background, he expressed frustration that people could not understand him, and that was hampering his efforts to share the gospel and make connections. I suggested that he listen to the pace and rhythm of the people around him, who were mostly speaking English, and that he imitate that. He became so proficient in speaking like a local that he drove his teammates crazy, but he made incredible connections, and is still remembered fondly years later.

CHAPTER 10F

PRACTICAL IMPLICATIONS OF SEEING OR JUDGING: PICTURES

This may seem a little more practically-oriented then the rest of this book, but with good reason. I remember a billboard outside an international airport about how for the rest of your life you can be the person that says, "Oh when I was in…" and it is true. Travelling to new and different places is an amazing thing. I have been to Africa more than twenty times, and have been in more than forty countries altogether, but I am still as excited as a child when I am getting ready to go.

I include this segment because it can ruin the experience and the connection with the culture if mishandled. I was in Eastern Europe once with a group that wanted to see a well-known and quite spectacular cathedral. Inside there were people quietly praying, but the group I was with paid them no mind as they gushed loudly and ran around taking pictures. I felt uncomfortable, and I moved back toward the exit. A young man who had been sitting and praying stopped as he reached the exit, spat bountifully in my face, and spoke what I can only assume was not a nice word. I have had manure and rocks thrown at vehicles I was in because team members took pictures without respecting the culture, and have seen a mild-mannered local pastor's wife almost strike a team member who was ignoring the instructions on when and where to take photos.

Picture-taking is a necessary part of being in another culture, both for memory's sake and for the required reports for donors and supporters back home. It is also helpful to defeat negative stereotypes of what the world is like, and to show the realities you experienced, not to mention the cool bragging rights when you hang that perfect picture on your office wall: "Oh yes, I took that myself, when I was in Africa..."

Be sensitive to local norms as to what is appropriate with picture-taking, and how you use the pictures later. The world is a small place, especially in this day and age of digital connection, and you do not know if the person in your photos might actually see it someday, and read what you wrote about them. Some may resent you taking their picture to use to promote your own work. I have seen other people use my pictures to promote their own ministry. My wife was quite surprised one day to see a picture of a missionary singing next to her, with a description of how this missionary is the worship leader in the church, which was my wife's title.

Also realize that people will judge you and your ministry by the pictures you post publically or in social media. If all your pictures are of you with a group of similar-looking foreigners on vacation, supporters might (and should) start to question your calling. Think about what story you want your pictures to tell, and if your pictures actually live that story out so they tell the truth. If you want a beautiful intimate photo of yourself arm-in-arm with your dearest foreign friend, then make that kind of friend! I've been known to pictures of myself with total strangers and ask if anyone can tell the story of what is happening in the picture.

CHAPTER 10G

PRACTICAL IMPLICATIONS OF SEEING OR JUDGING: TOUCH

"Oh be careful little hands…" So often we unintentionally send the wrong message by who or what we are touching, or not touching. Be careful of misleading people with inappropriate touching. In a remote area a group was gathered around the fire, late at night, enjoying food and fellowship. The young American girl talked with her hands, and kept touching the arm or shoulder of the man seated next to her. After some time, she stood up and said she needed to use the facility. The man took what was to him an obvious cue, preceded by some obvious seduction, and stood up to follow her. Thankfully several of the group were aware and alert, and made him sit back down. The girl had no clue.

There is a thought-provoking occurrence in the TV show "Outsourced"[xv] in which an American manager is trying to run a call center in India. As he walks around the room, he casually touches people or makes comments and gestures that are seemingly innocuous in his cultural view, but make him appear to his Indian employees to be a horribly uncouth person.

At the same time, be aware that not touching people

can send a negative message as well. Avoidance of a handshake can be interpreted as an unwillingness to touch someone with a certain skincolor, or from a certain tribe or social class. I, like many others, have had some embarrassing moments while in cultures that kiss on the cheeks, in not quite knowing which way to go and when.

The key here is intentionality. In the same way that we are admonished to guard our tongues, we must be aware of where our hands are and what they are doing. Our body language can send clear signals that we are utterly unaware of. I think of the lady that visited my in-law's home, and immediately propped her feet up on the table, which is where the family serves their food. On the flip side, intentional touching can be a breakthrough in cultural connections. In some cultures, men hold hands as a sign of friendship, and though my middle school self was laughing at me, I have walked through many public places holding hands with another man. In disaster response, a timely hug can open up a floodgate of tears, and an incredible chance to share the gospel.

If you are in a cross-cultural context and find yourself falling in love with a person from the local community, good for you! My wife and I are married cross-culturally, and God has blessed our marriage tremendously. When this is happening, though, you must seek advice from older and wiser believers. Specifically try to find someone else who has married into that culture, and begin to meet with them early in your relationship.

There are many cultural norms and taboos when it comes to dating, and specifically in how you touch each other in public. While an exchange student in an African university, I heard the school chaplain give a strong warning in chapel about the evils of men hugging women in public, and how this was becoming a plague among the young students. I was one of the most guilty, having also been one to give hugs. In some stricter cultures, the simple act of a man walking alone with a woman is enough for the families to demand they marry.

CHAPTER 10H

PRACTICAL IMPLICATIONS OF SEEING OR JUDGING: WORSHIP

The Kenyan church in which my wife, Hellen, led worship was an intentional cross-cultural effort by Africans to reach into the existent local Asian community. If you study the history of East Africa, you realize this is complex and a bit revolutionary. Some eleven language groups were represented on any given Sunday, and so music would often be sung in each language. Several of the cultures represented incorporate dancing as part of their traditional worship, and so a Bhangra or other such dance is not uncommon. Hellen and I were still dating, and I had brought a team to work in support of the church's ministries, and had told them the expectations I had for them in terms of following the lead of the local culture in order to strengthen their time of ministry. I, of course, was also trying to show off how great I was at cross-cultural ministry. Hellen was leading an Indian song, and everyone got up to dance. I am a terrible dancer, but I moved up to the front. As I reached the front, a majority of the congregation moved the other direction in a conga-line type dance, leaving me stranded with a few others. I desperately looked around for someone to imitate. The pastor is an amazing dancer, and was doing all these complex arm waves, Hitch-style lightbulb changing moves. No help there. A young man was doing some kind of ghetto roll back move, and a missionary couple was waltzing together (mad bonus points to them for a creative response). One local church member was there, and seemed to be lifting his arms up and then bringing them back down to his waist. This I could do, so I began to imitate him, feeling pretty good about myself, until I saw the look on Hellen's face, clearly begging me to stop. After the service, I was walking around the back of the church and I heard that same men telling his friends how he had forgotten his belt, and had to keep pulling his pants up while dancing. There was much laughter, and to this day the men of the church honor me with a special "pants" dance when I visit.

Yes, it may be way outside your comfort zone, but follow the local cultural norms when it comes to worship, providing of course that they are not sinful. If there is dancing, get your feet moving; if there is clapping, clap away. Not participating may make you look hostile to the culture, or judgmental of the church. You may want to ask ahead of time, and bring some water with you. Once in South Sudan we ended up jump-dancing for several hours, and that was just a greeting.

Historically missionaries have gotten sidetracked by the form of worship, rather than the content. You can find churches all over the globe that look just like an old-fashioned western church service, but don't preach the gospel at all. I am not delving into doctrinal issues here, but simply talking about how to respond when visiting churches in a different cultural setting. There is a time and a place for dialogue about what happens in a worship service, but do not use the actual time of worship for your protest.

CHAPTER 11

MINISTRY OR SAFETY?

"Do not fear, for I have redeemed you; I have summoned you by name; you are mine. When you pass through the waters, I will be with you; and when you pass through the rivers, they will not sweep over you. When you walk through the fire,
you will not be burned; the flames will not set you ablaze. For I am the Lord your God, the Holy One of Israel, your Savior." Isaiah 43:1-3.

I think this is a scripture passage that many mission trip leaders fear. It's not that we doubt the words, or the power of the Almighty to save, it's just that we need people to be wise. Most places in the world have great hospitals, but I would far prefer not spending time in them. We go with great confidence, knowing the Lord is with us, but we are also called to be wise. Often while doing ministry, you will be put in places where you need to make a decision about what is more important to you: ministry or safety.

In the mid 1990's I worked with a HIV/AIDS ministry, at a time when things were just beginning to change with treatment of the disease but also with the Christian world's perspective on affected and infected persons. I was sent to visit a man on his deathbed, something we did far too often in those days. I knew this man by reputation, and had never heard anything good said about him. As I walked into his room, he stuck his hand down his pants, and then held that hand out for me to shake, looking me in the eyes with a smirk on his face. I did not hesitate, but grabbed his hand. As soon as I left the room I scrubbed that hand as hard as I could. Another time I was doing disaster response work in an area where we were closely guarded by anti-Christian soldiers. We were cautious in our interactions with them, maintaining a careful distance. One day they showed up with a number of fresh local fruits, and proceeded to chop them up using their machetes, and then brought them to us as a gift. We knew full well they were not clean or safe to eat, and some chose to walk away, but some of us felt the ministry opportunity was too important to pass up, so we ate. We got sick and I don't think the soldiers got saved, so I am not sure if we made the right decision or not.

You know full well that sacrifice is required of you on the mission field, and it has probably been drilled into you that sacrifice does not mean stupidity. Be safe, and be smart, but know that sometimes you will have to make difficult decisions about what is best for your ministry, and what is the smart, safe thing to do. Be creative in finding ways around this, and remember that God is sovereign, no matter what you decide.

It is also important to remember that the freedom to make the decision between safety or ministry may not be yours to make, or may not be for you to make for yourself alone. In a team context this will generally fall to the leadership, and if you are the leader you have to factor in the overall safety and strength of the team. If one team member gets ill or in trouble, that will impact and limit the entire team: their time, their ministry, and their finances. The local church or community leadership may also be far stricter than you personally would be, and you must submit to their authority. While travelling solo I was often given strict curfews, boundaries, and restrictions by the people I was staying with or working under, and had to respect that.

CHAPTER 12

PERCEPTION OR INTENTION?

"It's easy to throw the baby out with the bathwater when it comes to Apartheid," the white missionary stated from the pulpit of our racially-mixed church. As a member of the missions committee I was tasked with following up after this statement, which caused great offense to many in our congregation. The missionary was so angry that we would question his statement and especially that it would have implications for his future financial support, and continued to repeat that we were misunderstanding his intention in making that comment.

Somehow in our society it has become the acceptable norm that our intentions are more important than another's perception of our words or actions. If confronted about making an offensive or inappropriate remark, the casual response is often something along the lines of: "Well, I am sorry that bothers you, but you misunderstood my intention. I am saying that this is not the proper response, but rather is simple blame-shifting.

Let's keep in mind a few scriptures:

"All things are lawful," but not all things are helpful. "All things are lawful," but not all things build up. Let no one seek his own good, but the good of his neighbor." 1

Corinthians 10:23-24.

"Put on then, as God's chosen ones, holy and beloved, compassionate hearts, kindness, humility, meekness, and patience, bearing with one another and, if one has a complaint against another, forgiving each other; as the Lord has forgiven you, so you also must forgive. And above all these put on love, which binds everything together in perfect harmony. And let the peace of Christ rule in your hearts, to which indeed you were called in one body. And be thankful. Let the word of Christ dwell in you richly, teaching and admonishing one another in all wisdom, singing psalms and hymns and spiritual songs, with thankfulness in your hearts to God. And whatever you do, in word or deed, do everything in the name of the Lord Jesus, giving thanks to God the Father through him." Colossians 3:12-17

"If your brother sins against you, go and tell him his fault, between you and him alone. If he listens to you, you have gained your brother." Matthew 18:15

There is a common theme in these verses, and throughout the Scriptures, in how we should interact with each other. Often we tend to extremes: we either say nothing and let sin continue or bitterness take root; or we are quick and harsh to point out the wrongs of others. I confess my tendency to do both: often my fear of responding harshly inhibits me from responding at all. We need to speak out, to point out wrongs and sinful behavior, and in the cross-cultural contact this becomes essential. We do not know we are doing wrong sometimes unless it is pointed out to us, but then when it is pointed out our response becomes defensive. "You don't understand!" we bark back, or, "I only had good intentions."

Our response rather must be marked by love. A simple apology will go a long way, and then hopefully some self-analysis that leads us to make the changes or adjustments that can take place. When we try to defend another's bad perceptions of our good intentions, we are simply telling that person that they are the one who is in the wrong, that the sin is against us in if they don't understand that we meant no harm. As Christians, as with travelers who are passing through, we often have only that brief interaction to make some impression. If our goal in all we do is to exemplify Christ, to be the aroma of Christ, than we must be aware of how our words and actions are perceived.

Too often I have heard stories, often from indigenous leaders, of a foreign visitor being confronted with a concern about their behavior and responding to that criticism with either a lofty justification of their own good intent, or by a dismissive shrug. When you make a mistake, or cause a hurt, or unknowingly, unintentionally, and unwillingly offend, let love guide your response. Say you are sorry for causing offense, apologize for what you did, and learn from it. After a sincere apology, you may have a chance to ask about what you did and why it caused problems. Be willing to be wrong, which is so hard for me and many from my culture. Be willing to accept a rebuke, even when you know your intentions were good, and remember that often the perception of your action is all that a stranger may have to go by, and you will be judged accordingly.

CHAPTER 13

EMPATHY OR SYMPATHY?

In John 11 we find the story of the death of Lazarus. Lazarus is a friend of Jesus, and much loved by many of His followers. When Lazarus dies, Jesus delays in coming, but when He does come, He sees Mary weeping and is deeply moved: "When Jesus saw her weeping, and the Jews who had come with her also weeping, he was deeply moved in his spirit and greatly troubled." John 11:33. Jesus is so moved, He weeps. Because Jesus has become fully man, and walked and fellowshipped with these people, He is connected to them at a deeper level. If He were doing a slide show of His time on Earth, there would definitely be some fun selfies with Mary, Martha, and Lazarus. This deeper connection leads Him to empathy, which is defined as "the ability to understand and share the feelings of another."[xvi] Sympathy is more an emotional response to the perceived suffering of others.

As children, we would say, "I'm not laughing at you, I'm laughing with you." Sympathy is showing emotion toward something; it is a one way street. Empathy is sharing emotions with someone; it goes both ways, and it involves actually understanding another's feelings. Empathy is one of the most powerful connections that can be made, and an incredible expression of the gospel. Sympathy can be an incredible turnoff ("I don't want your pity!") and make people feel demeaned. It can take a substantial amount of work to build the relationship or the connection for true empathy to happen.

I have often seen a team member on a short-term team who begins the trip cold and distant, and seems to be questioning or challenging everything, or complaining incessantly. Then, and too often towards the end of their limited time, a change occurs. They begin to smile, and often end the trip with some of the strongest long term relationships. The change comes because they actually got to know a person, and as they began to see this total foreigner as a real person, they experience a deep personal epiphany. They are not always aware of it, but it is glaringly obvious to the team leaders and often to the community they are working in.

When doing disaster response there is an incredible opportunity to connect and share with people at a deeper level. In response to Katrina, often it was as simple as asking a stranger how they were doing, or stopping and asking someone how they had been affected. On the side of the road, in the long lines at the few open stores, and on three occasions in the bathroom, I had total strangers crying on my shoulder as I prayed for them and sought to speak words of support and encouragement.

A deeper level of knowledge about the culture can help bridge this gap, and open the door to these connections. Japan is in many ways a cold climate culture (for more information about hot and cold climate culture differentiation, see Sarah Lanier's book Foreign to Familiar):[xvii] people may not open up easily to outsiders, and tend to guard their emotions closely. I first came across the concept of weather impacting culture in some of Ali Mazrui's writings about snow and the impact it had on the development of first world countries. After the Tsunami in Japan, we sent a team to assist in a hard- hit community through a Japanese pastor that we knew. On the team were several women who had grown up either in Japan or in Japanese culture. These women in Japan had a tremendous impact because they already loved the people and understood the culture on a deep and personal level, and not only did it show, but it allowed them to empathize. We have a beautiful picture of one of these American ladies sharing with a Japanese woman, with her hand holding the face of the Japanese woman as they cry together.

CHAPTER 14

LEARNING OR IMPOSING?

We do not go to make the world American, nor do we go to fix everything that is broken. We go to make disciples, and to do this effectively, we must have a learner's heart, seeking to know the culture and the people better, so we can relate better, so we can share deeper, so we can truly be a brother or sister in Christ. Always be looking for what God has to teach you.

While a student at an African university, I struggled to understand the norms when it came to time. It often seemed that time was irrelevant, but at other times it was essential. A professor who was never on time for anything would berate and even remove a student who came late for class. Somehow the schedule worked, and one class would end and another begin. There was a tea time between classes, and as I drank my tea the professor from my next class joined me, and we entered into a lively discussion. Ironically, we were talking about the norms of African culture versus Western culture. I was facing the classroom, while he had his back to it. I could see all of my fellow students already in the room, and yet our conversation continued for quite some time. He seemed in no rush to stop our conversation, and the class sat and patiently waited for us to finish. I know in the U.S. the class would have left after ten minutes or so. When our conversation came to a natural conclusion, he turned and we walked into class together, and he began the lecture with no explanation or apology. It was a great experience for me in realizing that sometimes I simply will not understand the cultural norms, and feeling humbled that the professor viewed spending time conversing with me as a priority, even if that was possibly just because I was a white American. A few weeks later he said something I disagreed with, and I questioned him in front of the class. That was a no-no, and I saw a very different side of the system.

One of my favorite things over the many years I have been involved in missions and cross-cultural ministry is learning from folks that are different from me, and particularly having conversations about those differences, and how to better work together. I encourage you to seek out people to learn from, particularly older folks who have seen and experienced things long-since relegated to the history books. Invite them out for coffee or lunch, and hold your tongue – this is not the time for you to tell your stories or make your points, just listen and soak it in.

Ephesians 5:21 tells us to submit to each other in reverence for Christ. As you go, there are great and exciting things out there. Go with a learner's heart. Don't go to impose your way of doing things on others, or to force others to your cultural views.

In one of my early trips to Africa, I met an older man who was giving us some wisdom before we departed, and I have never forgotten his words. I have tried hard to follow his advice, and it has served me well. "While you are here, in Africa, you will have seen good things and bad things. Some very good, and maybe some very bad. When you go, leave the bad things here with us. We know them, we are used to them, and we know how to deal with them. Take only the good things with you."

CHAPTER 15

STEWARDSHIP

Is missions still worth the money? There are big issues to be wrestled with in how we continue to do missions, both short- and long-term. I recently was approached to help provide administrative assistance to a group of eighteen pastors whose collective annual financial need was less than three thousand dollars, and a few weeks earlier had met with a young couple needing to raise more than twelve thousand dollars per month! Steve Saint, in his book <u>End of the Spear</u>,[xviii] has some great observations on how to do missions. I personally am convinced that the new mission field needs to involve job creation, and not just on a microeconomic existence level. Eternal hope is one of the great things we as Christians offer, but I want to see us helping poor people believe there is hope that they will not always live their lives on the brink of poverty. Everywhere I go both in the U.S. and abroad I meet incredible young people in the churches who are not able to get decent jobs, and I feel like we need to be helping them have a chance at a better tomorrow. Imagine what could happen if missionaries raised less for themselves and their administration, and instead raised funds to start businesses that gave young people in the church and community a real career.

In a recent missions meeting, the question was asked whether prayer support or financial support of missionaries was more important. It was a difficult question to answer because, although everyone believed the correct biblical answer was that prayer was more important than financial support, everyone wanted to add a qualifier to their response. Our own recognition of our reliance on the financial support others give influenced our response to the question. Our sinful nature and weak flesh lead us to think primarily of our physical needs, and we know our own financial struggles, but we need to encourage deeper probing of our own thoughts and hearts if we are to more fully realize our faith and live the life to which Christ is calling us.

There are two areas I want to look at in relation to stewardship. The first is how we view and utilize local resources, and the second is how we use our resources in missions and ministry. It has often been said that we'd be better off just raising and sending money to the local church, rather than raising the funds to send people. I disagree with this for three reasons. First, I believe that ultimately our calling is to discipleship, which means relationships, which best occur face to face. Second, I think that when we look at the ministry of Paul and the early church we see the value they place on being connected physically: even when writing letters Paul shows that his preference is to be there in person. Third, money tends to follow people, and while a team may spend large amounts of money in getting to the field they can be a tremendous financial blessing to the local church and community, so that even if they make a mess culturally or otherwise, the local ministries are still blessed.

Utilizing local resources is an essential part of

stewardship and will also help us in our attempt to develop deeper connections with the culture and community. I look at the budget of every trip and try to figure out how I can spend every possible dollar in a way that benefits the church and the community. As often as possible we will try to have teams hosted by local church members, and then pay them the money we would have spent on hotels or guest houses, or look for a ministry that has the facilities to house visitors so that the money goes to their ongoing work. For food, we will often hire local church or community members to cook for us, which puts money in their pockets, supports the local markets, and gives visitors a more authentic culinary experience. I ask around to see who owns or is connected to restaurants, taxis, safari companies, etc. As is standard in many large development organizations, we try to hire local help to travel with the teams. Hiring the youth or unemployed workers from a church or community gives you a tremendous connection, is a blessing to all involved, and might just help someone get a long-term job.

On a more personal level, think about how you can be a good steward of the money you are carrying and the things you have with you. Don't bring your junk to give away, but do think about giving away everything you bring with you. Be generous to a fault, but use discretion in doing this. Be reckless, but not foolish. Deacons were ordained in the church to handle distributing gifts to the poor, so when working with a local church ask about giving through the Deacons. One team member stayed with a family that needed a refrigerator due to health needs of a young child. I connected her to the Deacons of the church the host family attended, and not only were they excited to be involved but they contributed additional funds and helped the family buy an even better fridge. On another trip, a team member wanted to help pay for a surgery needed by a woman in the community, and the Deacons were called and asked for guidance.

Work through local resources, always, and follow their suggestions. Do not hand out cash because you feel bad about someone's situation, but give that cash through the church or community leadership. Don't give all your clothes to some poor person, but rather to the director of a school or orphanage, or to someone in the church who runs a small shop selling used clothes.

Hire personal shoppers to help you both with supplies and with the requisite tourist gifts. We often will ask young people to go with our teams on shopping days, and pay them for their time. They usually will help you get better gifts for less money, the experience of shopping together is likely to be unforgettable for all involved, and the gifts that much more special. I was looking for something to bring to my wife while in Haiti after the earthquake, and saw a young woman from the church wearing a beautiful straw hat. I gave my Haitian friend money, and asked if he could find one for her. He looked hard, and ended up not finding that hat, but another nice one. I thanked him, and my wife loved it. The next time I was in Haiti he met me at the airport holding the hat I had wanted, as he had gone back to the young lady and she had shown him where to buy it. A simple gift became one of great significance, and benefitted all involved.

CHAPTER 16

THE KEYS TO THE KINGDOM

A new person shows up, the "Super Volunteer" we all dream of. They are excited, energetic, full of ideas and spiritual fervor. Within weeks we have handed them the keys to the kingdom. We might do a token check on their background, but rarely do we actually do any research or spend much time or money on digging deeper. We can see how sincere and genuine they are, plus they are solving problems we long ago lost energy for dealing with. I have seen this happen time and time again, and have often been guilty of this myself. I have seen programs and even strategies tossed aside to cater to this new "Super Volunteer", especially if they have that magical combination of being an enthusiastic volunteer and the appearance of financial generosity.

We generally make two mistakes. The first is that we often are not providing the mentoring, support, and long-term attention that that will convert this wild-eyed radical into a long-haul veteran. The second is that we are quick to hand off responsibility without really ensuring that this is the right person, and end up a little ways down the road with a mess on our hands.

We are so busy: the harvest is plentiful and the workers are few. When this new person comes along we let them take as much as they want, and often end up burying them in the process. I know I have burned out my share of helpers, or let them get so overwhelmed that they end up quitting. I also have seen so many eager beavers come and go that sometimes I just don't want to bother putting the time in once again to get to know them, build the relationship, and slowly bring them down the road to responsibility.

At the same time, because they want it, we let them have it. A friend of mine calls it handing them the keys to the kingdom, and often the buildings, vehicles, and just about everything else as well. Too often we get burned in doing this. A recent story from Kenya tells of a young American teenager who abused multiple children sexually while volunteering at an orphanage. This is an extreme situation, and one of our worst fears, but we if we are honest we make ourselves vulnerable to this over and over. We need to be patient, and put good policies in place.

We need to be careful even in who we send on mission trips, and many of the same concerns apply, as they so often will work with children, and often in a situation where there is little supervision. When a new person comes along, whether to our ministry or to participate in a trip, and especially one who wants to work with our children or youth, conduct a thorough background check, and let them start with lesser responsibilities. Ask them to come help set up chairs, or cook food. If they want assist in transportation, first require them to ride along with an established helper, and then make sure they are always accompanied while picking people up. Slowly increase their leadership responsibilities, while getting to know them and their capabilities, and watch for unusual behavior. One thing I have often seen is people who act friendly around kids or youth, but are uncomfortable or even antisocial around groups of adults. Teach them how to run programs, and how to take responsibility for the kids in their care. It may be advisable to ask them to wait a year or two before going on a trip or doing external ministry work. Doing this slowly and intentionally will both help you create long-lasting reliable volunteers and help protect you and the children entrusted to your supervision. A key here is to encourage the mentorship and grooming of young people for ministry before they go to the mission field. Do it at home first, because if you are not doing it at home, you are not likely to do it on the mission field.

CHAPTER 17

FEEDBACK IS ESSENTIAL

When done properly, a short-term mission trip should leave both sides hungry for more: more time, more interaction, more ministry, more fellowship. This is because we were made to be connected, to be together. We are family, we are the global body of Christ, and we need each other.

A vast majority of the cultural struggles we have seen come because people are not seeking out genuine feedback from the culture they are working with. This goes along with making friends, for, as Tim Keller puts it: "Like a surgeon, friends cut you in order to heal you."[xix] You need to build up friendships to a point where people will feel able to be honest and direct with you, but encourage this by regularly asking local church leaders and your local friends how you are doing. Ask for suggestions on what you can do better, or areas that are problematic, and humbly accept the responses you receive.

We still follow the missions model developed over a hundred years ago, which is that of the international (foreign) missions organization sending people into another place. For some reason, this is still often done outside of the local existing churches or without consultation with the community leadership. This is not our fight, and there is little you can do about that in your context, but if we can learn from the mistakes of the past, we might be able to do things better going forward. It astonishes me that people do not ask the local leadership for feedback. Millions of dollars are spent every year in missions, and yet we are failing to get legitimate feedback from the very people we are supposed to be working with. I feel like this is common sense, and is a common practice and understood reality in the business or corporate world. Every restaurant I go to seems to want me to fill out a survey, and I get emails almost every day asking for my opinion on something or another. The very simple question "How are we doing?" is so powerful, and prevalent in so many aspects of life, but strangely absent when it comes to cross-cultural situations.

In running a missions committee, I rarely am able to see feedback on how our missionaries are actually doing. The few reviews I do see are peer reviews, done almost exclusively by fellow missionaries or expatriates. If pushed, I might be given something from a local who is either employed by or otherwise financially dependent on the good will of the foreigner, and thus I don't put much stock in the legitimacy of the feedback. Maybe we can create anonymous surveys for local church or community members to fill out, asking the simple "How are we doing?" question. The lack of feedback hinders progress in missions and world evangelism, and keeps us from a more strategic approach to missions and international response.

We have had teams go out and encounter serious issues that have necessitated action from the Session or mission board back home. We have had missionaries say things in the pulpit or other speaking engagements that betray the true character of how they actually function. My wife, who is African, sat in a chapel service at a Christian college and heard the visiting missionary use the word "savages" in reference to the people he worked with in another part of Africa. She walked out, and a dozen others followed, but several hundred did not. A visiting missionary in a church with a diverse racial membership condoned apartheid, and another spoke of how most of the local people where he worked were liars and thieves. We try to push, to ask hard questions about who their friends are, how and where they spend their time, and what they are learning from the culture, and we monitor social media to see what they are showing about themselves, but really we have little information. So this is a problem not only on an institutional level but also on a personal level.

Find someone to give you feedback, a local (indigenous) person who has nothing to lose by telling you the truth. Maybe it is a total stranger that you see on a regular basis, and you simply walk up and ask how they think you are doing. I was blessed to be able to study overseas, and my fellow students were quite happy to point out all I was doing wrong, often to their own great amusement. After the earthquake in Haiti we saw many organizations building all kinds of shelters, or trying to do things to help, but so often they were not getting local feedback, and when they were it was from people who stood to benefit greatly by saying the right things. Houses were built that no sane person would ever live in. After Hurricane Katrina we saw massive piles of clothing rotting in parking lots, donated by well-intentioned folks around the country and sent down with no plan or contact on the ground, and so the truck drivers simply dumped it where they could. Policies are drawn up in fancy offices, books written from comfortable classrooms, and money sent without impact or accountability, but feedback from the other side is rarely factored in.

I have been training teams for many years now, and once in a while people actually listen to me. We had taken a team to Kenya and on the team was a man who is a dearly beloved friend of mine. He was used to speaking to groups in the U.S. and had previously done some preaching, so we had prepared him that he would likely be called upon to preach or share at various points in the trip, as this was a normal occurrence. He had gone through the basic training which we require of all teams, including a section on getting feedback. His first opportunity to speak was at an elementary school. We went for lunch afterward, and several of the Kenyan young people from our church were there. He asked them how he had done, and after a little uncertainty, they told him that he spoke too fast, and was hard to hear, and used words not familiar to them, and basically just had not done a good job. He was rather taken aback, and had to take a moment to swallow his pride, before asking for advice on what else he could do. A few days later he was asked to preach, and again asked the same young folk for feedback. They were effusive in their praise: his words were clear and the message was relevant, encouraging, and led people to respond. In the congregation that day were several visitors whom I knew not to be believers, and some of them later became Christians, though I cannot say what role his words played in that.

I grew up in a log cabin in upstate New York, not the most diverse of upbringings, and in my late twenties found myself working at a church doing urban inner-city ministry. One of the first things I did was to seek out several African American friends who had grown up in this type of neighborhood, and ask them for two things: advice on how to do my job well, and a smack anytime I said or did things that could be perceived as inappropriate, inconsiderate, or even straight up racist. I got smacked a few times. After only a few weeks I got into trouble. In the job description some boundaries had been set, and based on those I said no to helping with a particular neighborhood event. My predecessors had always helped with this event, but it now fell under a different department. The leader of this event called me out at a community meeting, stating that she was surprised the church would hire one of those white racists. Immediately, two people who knew me stood up to my defense, and explained that this was not the case at all. My boss called me in the next day, and asked me a surprising question. "Well, are you a racist? No? Then prove it."

I hear stories of missionaries struggling with loneliness, and missionary kids feeling isolated from both their home and host cultures. I see missionaries who have been on the field for decades and are frustrated at how little fruit they are seeing. I see teams and visitors doing more harm than good, and though I remain a steadfast supporter and encourager of short-term trips, some of them really should have just stayed home and sent the money. At the same time I see people dwelling happily in foreign lands, loving and loved by the people they serve, and having effective and impactful ministry. I can't help but think that if everyone working in a cross-cultural context would take this advice to heart we would see radical change.

CHAPTER 18

PRAYER AND DISCIPLESHIP: THE REAL GREAT COMMISSION

Matthew 28:19, Acts 1:8, Luke 10:2, and Matthew 9:38 are some of the great classic missions texts, and have long been proclaimed loudly from pulpits and mission recruiters. "Go Ye into All the World" says the big banner, or "The Harvest is Plentiful, But the Workers Are Few." We have seen them a thousand times, and probably even said them ourselves, but so often we are missing key parts of those verses, and it changes the way we approach missions.

Prayer is too often underrated in our church, personal, and missional life. So often we plunge into things without pausing for even the briefest prayer. I remember the last game of high school basketball I ever coached. We had lost in the semifinals, and were playing the ever-dreaded third place consolation game. We had a tough season, but a good one. We came from behind, snuck into the playoffs, and almost had it all. We beat a much better team by hanging in and scoring a movie-quality last-second improbable basket, and lost a hard fight to the eventual champions on their home court. More than that though, I had worked hard with the guys to try to teach the more important things, to disciple them and to walk honestly with them, trying to live out my faith while building or encouraging theirs. That final game though we were all a bit down, frustrated and discouraged, and the game was ugly and not much fun. At halftime I did not have any great speeches or inspiring monologues, but then one of the younger player spoke up. "Coach," he said, "we didn't pray before the game, and I think we need it. Can we pray now?" Such a simple thing, and it did make a big difference. I'm not saying we won because we prayed, or implying that we were somehow more spiritual than the other team, but our attitudes changed.

We have two daughters, and both pregnancies had difficulties. Our eldest is named Niya, which means "purpose," because we knew God had a purpose for her life due to the things we went through in our lives and in that pregnancy. Our youngest is Sameera, which means "tranquility," because God gave my wife a tremendous sense of peace in the midst of that pregnancy.

It was almost time for Sameera to be born, and we went to the doctor for a final checkup and ultrasound. There was a different ultrasound tech, and when she looked at the pictures she panicked, which led to the midwife panicking, and on down the line. It seemed to her as if the baby was too big, and so they recommended an immediate induction and warned us to prepare for an emergency C-section. Then they realized they had to wait four more days before she was officially full term, so they told us to go home and come back at exactly midnight on the fourth day. What a stressful day that was. We fought over little things, we got all kinds of conflicting advice and input from friends and others, but we did not stop to pray. At around ten that night we remembered to pray, and we prayed for the baby's safety, for my wife's health, and for wisdom and guidance. I clearly remember just asking God to bring the baby now, even tonight, and just not even have to deal with these doctors. An hour later we were headed to the hospital, and a few hours after that the birthing nurse delivered a perfectly healthy baby. When we call on His name He hears us!

One of the first mission trips I ever helped lead was to an African country emerging from a long and horrid war. I had been there two years before, and thought I was just assisting on this trip, but ended up being the main leader for much of the trip, with a group of thirty high school students. We were stuck in a bad place, waiting for our bus to be repaired with parts that needed to be brought in from another country. Several people were sick, some with dysentery and others with malaria. We were staying in tents, on a hill overlooking a small town. The field we were staying on was the site of one of the biggest battles of the war, and bullet casings covered the ground like pebbles. On the back on the hill was a marked mine field, and further up the hill was an old building occupied by soldiers from the rebel army, who were still waiting to see if the cease-fire would hold, so they rolled out every morning with their automatic weapons to hunt the last remaining wildlife in a once-prosperous and plentiful game park.

We had several incidents of things being stolen from our camp, so I (and several guys from the local village) decided to stay up all night to keep watch. They promptly curled up in their blankets by the fire and went to sleep. I climbed to the top of the bus to keep watch, but it was very cold, so I crawled into my mummy-like sleeping bag. As I lay there, the ridiculousness of my situation struck me. I was powerless. It would take me several minutes to wiggle my arms back out of the mummy bag, and even then all I had was a wood club. I realized how dangerous things were, and began shaking with fear. I don't know how long I lay there paralyzed by terror before I remembered to pray. I prayed, a simple David-like cry for help, and several things happened. The first is that the stars poured down on top of me. There was a massive meteor shower which began at the precise moment I finished my prayer. In the dark lonely African night, with no artificial light anywhere around, it was astonishing, and at any other moment of my life it would have been one of the most incredible things I have ever seen, more so than Victoria or Niagara Falls or a thousand stunning sunsets or sunrises. At that moment it was like a hug from my Father in Heaven, a clear voice reminding me that He is real. At the same time, a story from Scripture came to mind, and I could see it clearly in my head. The hill I was on was ringed by mountains, their ridges barely perceptible in the night, but in my mind I saw the tops of them covered with chariots of fire. I slept soundly the rest of the night, and things began to change the next day.

Matthew 9:38 is not calling us to go out and glean those fields ripe for the harvest, nor is it asking us to send people to the mission field. It is quite simply and directly a call for us to pray to the Lord of the harvest to send out laborers to the fields. How do we miss that? We read through this recently with our missions committee and were strongly convicted to be more focused on prayer, and on calling our congregation to prayer.

As we encounter difficult situations in cross-cultural

settings, we must first pray. As we get to know other believers around the globe, our first interactions should be in prayer. It is so easy to get caught up in being busy and trying to do things, but let's take time and prioritize prayer. I have said for years that I only learned to pray when I went to Africa, and heard how the people there pray. That prayer could be so passionate, so song-like, was not something I had even imagined. I have been blessed to travel to many places and difficult situations, and in that have basked in some of the most incredible prayer times. Often there is nothing I can do to help or change a bad situation, a difficult life, or an overwhelming disaster, but I can always pray. There are so many faces in my mind, friends all over the globe that I will likely never see on earth again, but I remember them, and in the sleepless nights or endless hours of uncomfortable travel I pray for them. I can see their faces still, and remember the times we shared and ministered together. Many of them I have not had contact with in too many years, and maybe they have already gone, but still I pray.

The second aspect of these missional verses, what we often call the Great Commission, is the actual call or command to go into all the earth, to the uttermost parts of the earth. We are called to be witnesses of Christ, and to go and make disciples. If we study Paul's approach to missions, it is never just a short-term response, not drive-by evangelism, but rather a long-term commitment which involved extensive follow up. Short-term response should never exist outside of the context of a long-term relationship. We are called to discipleship.

Discipleship is about mentoring, it's about building lasting relationships, and creating an interaction that allows deeper connection. It is easy to get caught up in doing things, or accomplishing goals, or pursuing glorious successes in our ministry, and to forget that ultimately this is our call. If our purpose in life is to worship God, then our call becomes to help others do the same.

This does not negate a call to be witnesses, to spread the gospel, but changes our approach to it, especially when coupled with an understanding of the sovereignty of God. Look at the parable of the sower. This is quite possibly the worst farmer ever, and if he worked for any of us would be fired immediately. I picture the flannelgrams of my childhood Sunday school classes, and here is the guy with a sling or satchel full of seeds, flinging them carelessly in all directions. In my memory I see him whistling as he goes. Some seeds fall on the path and are eaten by birds, some fall on rocks and thorns and die quickly as well. So maybe a quarter of the seeds he throws actually land in good soil. What a waste! We know better; we must be more efficient, better stewards of the resources given to us. It's not good economic policy to spend $3000 on a short-term mission trip we say, and it is much cheaper and more effective to only hire nationals to do ministry; let's stop supporting foreign missionaries. Thankfully the call to follow Christ is foolishness in the eyes of man, and thousands still do respond to the command to go and be witnesses. We must never stop, but let's try to do it better!

CHAPTER 19

CONCLUSION

I stated at the beginning that the solution was quite simple, and it really is. We need to become like children in the way we approach each other. I can think of countless times where I have seen spontaneous play break out between children who are total strangers, and it usually begins with one child asking the other a simple question: "What's your name?" or "How old are you? I'm five." A few minutes later they are lost in the make-believe play world, and are best friends.

The other amazing thing about how children approach each other is that they are not generally afraid of making mistakes. I think the fear of being embarrassed or feeling awkward inhibits us from action more than almost anything else. We may try to spiritualize our reluctance, or hide behind advanced rhetoric about being true our own culture, but the reality is we are just afraid that we will look like an idiot, or be ridiculed. It's okay. You will mess up, you will embarrass yourself, and you will be laughed at. You will order mud instead of bananas, you will unintentionally cause offenses, and you will make some great friends as a result, and start to see the barriers come down.

We need to be like this as adults. It really is as easy as

treating others the way we would like to be treated –
intentionally. It begins with walking up to a stranger,
especially one who is "different" from us, smiling, putting
out our hand, and saying, "Hello, I'm Brian. What's your
name?" Great things will follow.

You will come to a place where the streets are not marked.
Some windows are lighted. But mostly they're darked.
A place you could sprain both your elbow and chin!
Do you dare to stay out? Do you dare to go in?
How much can you lose? How much can you win?

And IF you go in, should you turn left or right...
or right-and-three-quarters? Or, maybe, not quite?
Or go around back and sneak in from behind?
Simple it's not, I'm afraid you will find,
for a mind-maker-upper to make up his mind...

And when you're alone, there's a very good chance
you'll meet things that scare you right out of your pants.
There are some, down the road between hither and yon,
that can scare you so much you won't want to go on.

But on you will go
though the weather be foul.
On you will go
though your enemies prowl.
On you will go
though the Hakken-Kraks howl.
Onward up many
a frightening creek,
though your arms may get sore
and your sneakers may leak.

On and on you will hike,
And I know you'll hike far
and face up to your problems
whatever they are. xx

103

CHAPTER 20

NOTES

[i] All scripture ESV (English Standard Version).

[ii] John Piper, "Becoming all things to all men to save some," Desiring God Foundation, 2015, 7 April 2015, <http://www.desiringgod.org/sermons/becoming-all-things-to-all-men-to-save-some>.

[iii] Anthony Bradley, "The New Legalism," World Magazine, 7 April 2015, <http://www.worldmag.com/2013/05/the_new_legalism>.

[iv] Piper.

[v] Mother Teresa, In the Heart of the World: Thoughts, Stories and Prayers (Novata, California, U.S.A.: New World Library, 1997).

[vi] Pastor Randy Nabors, Merciful (SC: CreateSpace Ind. Pub, 2015) <http://www.thenewcitynetwork.org>.

[vii] Richard D. Allen, The Genesis Principle of Leadership (Oklahoma: Tate Publishing & Enterprises, LLC, 2008) 21.

[viii] Brian Fikkert & Steve Corbett, When Helping Hurts: How to Alleviate Poverty Without Hurting the Poor . . . and Yourself (Moody, 2012) <https://www.chalmers.org>.

[ix] Francis Schaeffer, "How Should We Then Live?" FrancisSchaefferStudies.Org <http://francisschaefferstudies.org/home/works/francis-schaeffer/How-Should-We-Then-Live>.

[x] Jim Raymo, Marching to a Different Drummer (Ft. Washington, PA: Christian Literature Crusade, 1996) 95.

[xi] Alfred Ackley, "I Serve A Risen Savior," Hymnary.Org, April 2015 <http://www.hymnary.org/text/i_serve_a_risen_savior>.

[xii] Pastor Kevin Smith, New City Fellowship, Chattanooga TN. <http://www.newcityfellowship.com>.

[xiii] JRR Tolkien, The Lord of the Rings Trilogy (NY: Ballantine Books, 1970).

[xiv] Timothy Keller, Generous Justice: How God's Grace Makes Us Just (Dutton, 2010).

[xv] NBC, Outsourced <http://www.nbc.com/classic-tv/outsourced>.

[xvi] Miriam Webster "Empathy" <http://www.merriam-webster.com/dictionary/empathy>.

[xvii] Sarah Lanier, Foreign to Familiar (Hagerstown MD: McDougal Publishing, 2000).

[xviii] Steve Saint, End of the Spear (Tyndale Momentum, 2007).

[xix] Timothy Keller, The Meaning of Marriage: Facing the Complexities of Commitment with the Wisdom of God (Penguin Publishing, 2013).

[xx]Dr. Seuss. <u>Oh, the Places You will Go!</u> (NY: Random House, 1990).

ABOUT THE AUTHOR

Brian P. McKeon is the Founder and Director of R3
International. R3I seeks to meet needs in hard times and hard
places, with an emphasis on disaster response and cross
cultural training.
Brian has been involved in cross cultural ministry for over
twenty years, beginning with youth mission trips to Africa. He
has been a teacher, a missionary, a fire fighter, and a
lumberjack. At the time of writing, he is serving as a Deacon
at New City Fellowship of Chattanooga, TN, and as Chairman
of the Missions Committee.